PORTLAND BASIN

Portland Basin
and the Archaeology of
the Canal Warehouse

Volume 1 in the Archaeology of Tameside series

By

Michael Nevell and John Walker

Tameside MBC

2001
Tameside Metropolitan Borough Council
The Archaeology of Tameside

Volume 1: Portland Basin and the Archaeology of the Canal Warehouse

ISBN 1 871 324 254

First published in 2001 by
Tameside Metropolitan Borough Council
with The University of Manchester Archaeological Unit

Typeset by Carnegie Publishing Ltd
Chatsworth Road, Lancaster

Printed by The Cromwell Press
Trowbridge, Wilts

Contents

Preface

This introduction to the Portland Basin, its canal warehouse and the canals of Tameside, is the first in a series of booklets designed to introduce to a wider public some of the most important archaeological and historical monuments in the Borough of Tameside. As such the series aims to provide an overview of the development of each site, and to assess its regional importance. Drawing upon the fieldwork undertaken by the University of Manchester since 1990 on behalf of the Tameside Metropolitan Borough Council, including original research undertaken specifically for each volume, and using the rich archives held by the Local Studies Library in Tameside, these booklets aim to provide the most up-to-date and authoritative guides to the borough's rich historical roots. The Portland Basin is an outstanding illustration of the innovative techniques and new industries introduced into the borough by the local pioneers of the Industrial Revolution at the end of the eighteenth century and beginning of the nineteenth century. The warehouse, which was built in 1834 and has a number of unusual design features, is now a museum of social and industrial history and is open to the public, free of charge.

Cllr S. Roy Oldham, CBE

C. Eng. M.I. Mech. E.

Executive Leader of the Council

Acknowledgements

The concept of the original *History and Archaeology of Tameside* volumes arose in the course of a meeting between the leader of the Council, Councillor Roy Oldham, then Director of the Greater Manchester Archaeological Unit Phil Mayes, then Director of Planning Mike Eveson and Local Studies Librarian Alice Lock. Councillor Oldham pursued his belief in the value of the work and a publication programme was designed to cover the history and archaeology of Tameside, and ancillary works such as the *Archaeology of Tamside* series. The responsibility for monitoring the progress of the commission for Tameside fell to Barry Delve, Head of Services (Learning and Information Services). His support and that of the staff of the Local Studies Library at Stalybridge are gratefully acknowledged.

Many individuals assisted in the research, writing and production of this volume. Thanks are due to all the owners and occupiers of canal warehouses in the North West surveyed for this work, in particular British Waterways who gave access to many key properties in Cheshire and Lancashire; the co-operation and overall enthusiasm were both vital for the purposes of the volume and refreshing for the authors. Background information on particular sites was supplied by the county archaeologists for Cheshire and Lancashire, The Boat Museum at Ellesmere Port, the National Monuments Record Centre in Swindon and David George, Chairman of the Manchester Region Industrial Archaeology Society, who also read an early draft of the text.

Thanks must also go to Robina McNeil the County Archaeologist for Greater Manchester, Norman Redhead the Assistant County Archaeologist for Greater Manchester, Mike Clarke, and Mike Haddon of the History Shop in Wigan without whose help and support this book would not have been possible.

Finally, thanks to all those involved in the production of the book; Ivan Hradil, who took most of the photographs and drew the line drawings; Catherine Mackey, who proof read the volume; and John Roberts and Peter Connelly who undertook drawing and research work. If we have missed any persons from this list, our apologies. A work such as this necessarily rests on the goodwill of many individuals. Any mistakes or omissions are, of course, the sole responsibility of the authors.

Michael Nevell BA, MPhil, DPhil
John Walker BA Hons, FSA
University of Manchester Archaeological Unit
Field Archaeology Centre
University of Manchester
February 2001

The Origins and Development of the Industrial Warehouse

Introduction

The Portland Basin Museum, which houses the remains of the Ashton New Wharf warehouse, lies at the junction of the Ashton and Peak Forest canals in Ashton-under-Lyne (Fig 1.1). Although these two transport networks were opened in 1796 and 1797 Portland Basin was not built until 1834. Designed and constructed by David Bellhouse & Co it was one of the largest canal warehouses of its type and one of the biggest buildings in the then booming cotton town of Ashton. Conceived as a multi-purpose warehouse it handled thousands of tonnes of goods each year, from cotton, coal and limestone to corn, carrots and candles, all designed to keep Ashton's growing population fed and clothed, its industries supplied with raw materials and its products distributed throughout Britain. As an archaeological monument type the canal warehouse was a product of the Industrial Revolution and was one of a number of warehouse types that developed from 1760 onwards. However, the origins of the warehouse as a recognisable building type lie much further back.

Roman and Medieval Origins

The warehouse developed as a means of long term safe storage for bulk goods. In Britain the origins of such storage buildings can probably been seen in the large grain pits and timber, four-post, granaries of the Iron Age hillfort. Whilst doubt still remains about the precise role and function of these structures, the first true warehouses in Britain were built by the Romans who developed a sophisticated distribution system across their empire using three main types of warehouse; for long-term storage; temporary storage for transhipment or redistribution; and for small-scale, private storage.

Most of the Roman storage facilities excavated in Britain were military granaries designed for long-term storage. These single storey buildings were typified by floors in cement, stone or wood which were raised on piers to allow adequate ventilation and to keep out

Fig 1.1 Britain's first and last canals. An aerial view of the Bridgewater Canal, the world's first industrial canal opened in the 1760s, where it crosses the Manchester Ship Canal, Britain's last substantial artificial waterway, opened in 1894, via the Barton Swing Bridge. This replaced the earlier 1760s Barton Aqueduct. The earlier eighteenth-century line of the Bridgewater Canal can be seen to the right. These two canals mark the beginning and the end of the artificial waterway era in Britain's industrial history and are thus monuments of national importance. Photograph Professor Barri Jones.

pests. These were usually long, narrow, buildings with external walls supported by buttresses to compensate for the large weight of grain within and a single loading bay in one of the gable ends. In North West England the granary at the Castleshaw fortlet in the southern Pennines is typical of such military structures; being a timber-framed building 13m long by 7.5m wide raised on thirteen rows of posts, six to each row, with a loading bay at the northern end facing onto the main road of the fortlet. It was later enlarged to 18.5m × 9m (giving an area of 166.5m²), the additional floor space required being supported on an extra row of stilts (Walker 1989). This compares with an average size of roughly 6m × 30m and an area of approximately 180m² at the South Shields Roman fort, in Newcastle, which unusually had 24 granaries by the mid-third century and appears to have been used as a supply base for the garrisons along Hadrian's Wall (Bidwell and Hodgson 1999, 314–6). Civilian, or urban, warehouses are harder to identify and although buildings in Chester and York have been suggested as granaries such an identification remains speculative (Milne 1985, 68–9). The largest such structures in the Roman Empire were found in Rome where, for instance, the Horrea Galbana, which was formed by a series of store rooms set around a series of internal courtyards, covered 21,000m².

Examples of transhipment storage buildings are very rare in Britain, but two Roman dock-side warehouses were excavated in London during the 1980s (Fig 1.2). The water-logged conditions along the banks of the River Thames meant that these timber, brick and stone structures survived up to several metres high. In plan form they were single storey, rectangular buildings with their long access aligned to the quay-front, whilst the river side was an open frontage supported by wooden columns. Each had a floor area of approximately 150m². Similar open area quayside warehouses with roofs supported by columns are known across the empire, from Lyons and Trier in France to the ports of Roman North Africa (Milne 1985, 68, 73). Although these building types disappeared with the collapse of the Roman Empire in the fifth century AD the needs of long- and short-term storage, especially during the transhipment of goods from water to land, meant that similar structures were developed again from the later medieval period.

Fig 1.2 Roman quayside warehouses in London (after Milne 1985, 74 ills). Plans of two Roman dock-side warehouses, excavated in London during the 1980s. The water-logged conditions along the banks of the River Thames meant that these timber, brick and stone structures survived up to several metres high. In plan form they were single storey, rectangular buildings with their long access aligned to the quay-front, whilst the river side was an open frontage supported by wooden columns. Each had a floor area of approximately 150m². This open-fronted building design occurs again from the sixteenth century, at first in quayside locations, later also on canal basins.

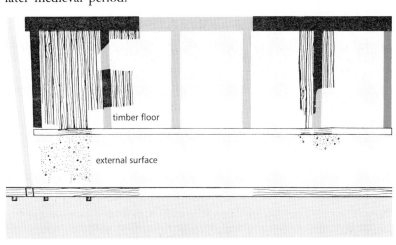

timber floor

external surface

During the medieval period warehouses again emerged as recognisable building types, for both long and short-term storage and they became in familiar feature of the medieval countryside. Barns, which were used for the long-term storage of a variety of produce but in particular grain, were a key part of the agricultural economy and were to remain so until the introduction of new forms of agricultural building in the twentieth century, such as grain silos. Like the Roman granary the medieval barn came in a variety of sizes, from small single storey barns used to store grain or stable livestock on a single farm (covering an area as little as two bays of approximately 50m²) to the large tithe barns, so-called after a local tax in kind of one tenth of local produce, which acted as collection and redistribution centres for large estates. The most recognisable of these new storage buildings was the monastic grange, or farm, and its tithe barn. The largest examples were usually aisled buildings of stone or timber, depending on the local materials available. The finest and most complete example of a monastic tithe barn in Britain is the huge barn at Great Coxwell, Berkshire, a timber and stone aisled building with a stone-tiles roof built as part of the grange serving the abbey at Beaulieu around 1300. The stone walls is 46.13m long, 13.4m wide and 14.6m high having a vast interior of *c.* 618m² which was approached through a central entrance in the gable end high enough for a loaded wagon (Brunskill 1994; Wilkinson 2000, 81). Such structures were multi-purpose buildings and used both for the processing of a variety of produce, but typically grain, as well as its long term storage and redistribution. Other fine examples include the barn at Leigh Court in Hereford and Worcestershire; a cruck building built by the Benedictine abbey of Pershore around 1300. It has eleven pairs of oak cruck trusses and is 46m long and 10m wide, giving a floor area of 460m² (Wilkinson 2000, 79). These large storage buildings would not be exceeded in size until the Industrial Revolution.

By the seventeenth- and eighteenth-centuries the functions of the barn had begun to separate so that many were used either for long term storage (of crops and livestock) or as processing and redistribution centres on the farm (Brunskill 1994; Peters 1969). In the North West there are still hundreds of barns surviving from this period, and although the combination barn dominates this group, specialised farm storage buildings were becoming increasingly common. These ranged in size from the small two bay cow house or shippon (as at Cinderland Hall in Tameside which had a single storey shippon with a floor area of *c.* 80m²) to large aisled threshing barns as at Warburton in Trafford, where a two storey brick barn built in 1714 had a floor area of 300m² (Burke and Nevell 1996, 48; Nevell 1997, 80). This growing separation of process, manufacture and collection was to become one of the characteristics of the industrial warehouse.

Coastal Ancestors

The direct ancestors of the canal and general purpose industrial warehouse lie in the sea and river ports of late medieval Britain where as early as the fifteenth-century merchants involved in overseas trade invested in impressive warehouses. Typically, they were located near to or on the quayside, as at Southampton, the greatest medieval port on the south coast and an important transhipment centre between England and France (Lloyd 1998, 114). Here the stone Wool House was built on the Town Quay around 1400 and had a number of typical warehouse features such as a long axis running away from the quayside, supported by large external buttresses and loading bay doors on the gable which fronted the quay; essentially this was a medieval quay-side barn. In Kings Lynn, Norfolk, one of the most important late medieval North Sea ports in England, such warehouses were set between the houses of the merchants who owned both them and the wharves. The timber-framed Hanse Warehouse, in St Margaret's Lane, was built by merchants of the Hanseatic League (an association of merchant guilds from cities in the Rhineland and the Baltic) in 1428 and used for over three centuries (Stratton and Trinder 1997, 90–1). An older style of warehouse can still be seen on the quayside at Exeter, where a stone and timber shed was built around 1680 by the city, using the stone foundations of an Elizabethan warehouse. It runs parallel to the water's edge and has a covered, open-sided, loading area on the quayside, reminiscent of Roman quayside warehouses. The rebuilt warehouse included a cantilevered roof to protect boats and cargoes (Stratton and Trinder 1997, 91).

Until the seventeenth century warehouses in Britain remained relatively small structures, but the growth of Britain's international trade and its overseas possessions led to a building boom from the commercial ports of Bristol, Liverpool and London and to the Royal Navy dockyards at Chatham and Portsmouth. In the late seventeenth and early eighteenth centuries the largest warehouses could be found at the latter two locations and were built by the Royal Navy to ensure that supplies were available in the event of war (Lloyd 1998, 184–5). The oldest surviving dockyard storehouse is the clock-tower building at Chatham built in 1723 but the stores at both Chatham and Portsmouth, where the latter survive from 1764 and 1784, contained many of the elements which would become familiar in the both the urban and waterside industrial warehouse; they were multi-storey, rectangular, brick buildings with arcaded ground floors with central pediments on each block and internally they had wooden floors and posts (Stratton and Trinder 1997, 91).

London had the largest grouping of dock-side warehouses in the eighteenth century. Here the building of such structures was prompted not only by the growth in overseas trade but also by the need to store goods in safety. Charters granted in 1661 and 1708 to the East India Company, which handled Britain's trade with Asia, granted the privilege of holding goods in bond deferring payment of import duty until they were ready for dispatch. During the eighteenth century other merchants gained this privilege on shipments of tobacco, rum, sugar and coffee and thus the London docklands were born. They were characterised by multi-storey brick warehouses, with taking-in doors, projecting hoists, internal timber floors and supports, each set around basins or along the river bank (Stratton and Trinder 1997, 91–3).

The Industrial Warehouses of the Eighteenth and Nineteenth Centuries

The huge city warehouses of the nineteenth century were a product of the new industrial urban society that emerged in Britain from the mid-eighteenth century onwards. By the 1840s the majority of Britain's population lived in the cities, rather than on the land. This divorce from the countryside and the agricultural cycle necessitated the growth of a sophisticated distribution system that could feed, cloth and keep warm the rapidly growing urban populations who earned their living in the factories or as middle-men. Central to this new distribution system was the warehouse. This was a period of major innovation in warehouse design spurred by two things; by the development of the new canal, rail and road transport networks and by the development of new power-systems coupled with the introduction of new building materials.

The first of these new warehouse designs was that of the canal warehouse. Although it owed much to its coastal predecessors in its most developed form it had a number of unique features, with internal water-filled canal arms, multi-storeys, split level loading, terracing and a hoist system run by water power. The first canal warehouse of this type was almost certainly the Duke's Warehouse in the Castlefield Basin of the Bridgewater Canal at Manchester, and was built 1769–71. It had the distinctive shipping holes, water-powered hoist system, split level loading and multi-storeys that quickly became the hallmark of this type of warehouse. This structure was demolished in 1960 but

Fig 1.3 The Remains of the Grocers' Warehouse, Castlefield, Manchester. The Grocers' Warehouse was largely demolished in 1960 and partially restored in the 1980s. Built in the early to mid 1770s this is one of the earliest canal warehouses built to the classic Type 1 design with internal water-filled canal arms, multi-storeys, split level loading, terracing and a hoist system run by water power. Other early examples of this type to survive include the 1777 terminal warehouse in Wigan on the Leeds and Liverpool Canal, Sir John Ramsden's Aspley Warehouse from the late 1770s built on the Huddersfield Broad Canal and a brick warehouse from 1780 in the canal town of Shardlow on the Trent and Mersey Canal.

the earliest surviving canal warehouses of this classic design date from the 1770s and include the remains of the Grocers' Warehouse (Fig 1.3), also at Castlefield in Manchester, and Ramsden's Aspley Warehouse, a multi-storey warehouse on the Huddersfield Broad Canal (Ransom 1979; Wilkinson 1980). The Portland Basin warehouse, although not built until 1834, follows this classical design, although it has a number of unusual design features, such as three internal canal arms, an external water wheel and a flat roof. There were also a variety of less sophisticated, smaller warehouse designs associated with the rural canal network. The usefulness of this classic design is shown by its adoption in each of the great cities of the Industrial Revolution; Birmingham, Glasgow, Leeds, Liverpool, London, Manchester and Sheffield.

Fig 1.4 The 1830 Railway Warehouse, Liverpool Road. The first railway warehouse in the world, built next to the Liverpool Road passenger station in Manchester. This warehouse borrowed a number of features used in contemporary canal warehouse design, most notably the use of split levels to reduce the transhipment problems.

The first railway warehouse was built in 1830 (Fig 1.4) and was attached to the Liverpool Road passenger station in Manchester. It was designed by Thomas Haigh, a Liverpool architect, who adapted designs he had produced for warehouses in the Gloucester Docks but which had not been built. These included the use of split levels to reduce the transhipment problems. Thus, the railway was two floors higher than the roadway mirroring the canalside/roadside single storey height difference that could be found in the largest canal warehouses of the period (Greene 1995a, 2–3). Other design features copied from contemporary canal warehouses included the use of wooden floors, cast-iron columns in the basement and wooden columns elsewhere, and the manual hoist system, although this was supplement in 1832 by steam; there being no convenient water supply for a waterwheel (Stratton and Trinder 1997, 97). Nevertheless, the Liverpool Road Warehouse had a number of unique features including its curving railway facade (Fitzgerald 1980; Green 1995b).

The introduction of cast iron-framing in the 1850s, and subsequently wrought iron and then steel framing, enabled the railway companies to build larger and higher warehouses than those next to the canals, and the use of these materials was also followed in the major ports of the country. Thus, in the second half of the nineteenth century the railway termini of the country were dominated by multi-storey square warehouse buildings, with iron, later steel, framing. In Manchester the 1869 bonded warehouse, which was built to the north of the Liverpool Road warehouse, and the London railway warehouse behind what is now Piccadilly station are two fine examples of this tradition. To these can be added the innovative quayside warehouses in Liverpool designed and built by Jesse Hartley between 1845 and 1860 and best exemplified by the Albert Dock with its curved iron roof and fireproof construction (Jones 1966) and the later Tobacco Warehouse with its austere elevations made possible by the steel-framing beneath its skin.

One result of the takeover of the canals by the railway companies was the construction of a number of combined canal/railway termini and warehouses, from the transhipment sheds at the southern end of the Peak Forest Canal at Buxworth in Derbyshire to the depots of the London and North Western and Great Northern Railways on the Regent's Canal in London (Fig 1.5). The Great Northern's depot had canal arms running into the basement whilst others ran alongside the transit sheds, the other side of which lay the railway sidings. The style and function of these wagon openings appear to have been inspired by the barge holes of the canal warehouse. Built in the years 1896–8 (Fig 1.6) the Great Northern Railway Warehouse,

Fig 1.5 King's Cross Goods Station, London. This view shows the canal, rail and road interchange built here in the mid-nineteenth century. The Great Northern Railway line is on the right, boats on the Regent's Canal can be seen in the centre and on the left are carts being loaded for delivery on the streets of London.

Fig 1.6 The Great Northern Warehouse, Manchester. This early steel framed building was built in the years 1896–98 by the Great Northern Railway Company as a road, rail and canal interchange. It heralded the beginning of the decline of canal freight transport and the rise of road haulage.

Manchester, represented the ultimate multi-purpose transhipment depot, combining road, rail and canal transhipment on five different levels. It encompassed state of the art construction technology, in the form of one of the first large steel-framed buildings in Britain, and there were hydraulic lifts which could move filled railway wagons from floor to floor.

A common feature of the industrial urban landscape was the private warehouse within a manufacturing complex. These followed in the tradition of the multi-storey canal warehouse and the early multi-storey railway warehouses and could be found within most large-scale nineteenth-century factory complexes, often being built on their own private canal arm or, later in the century, being served by their own railway sidings.

The most impressive urban warehouses of the nineteenth century were the commercial warehouses, typically built to service the textile industry. These became as much advertising symbols and state-ments of power and prestige as practical storage facilities. By the mid-nineteenth century groupings of private textile warehouses began to develop, characterised by elaborately ornamented facades, and notable warehouse quarters can still be seen in Bradford and Not-tingham (Stratton and Trinder 1997, 99–103). Manchester was already noted as a warehouse centre by the 1840s (Wilkinson 1980, 10–1) and as its commercial importance grew in the second half of the century so did the number of warehouses (McNeil and Nevell 2000, 9). Its architects pioneered the 'palazzo' or Italianate style of warehousing in the 1840s and 1850s, and this became a hallmark of the city. The steel-framed Manchester warehouses built between 1890 and 1914 marked the pinnacle of this type of warehouse, with structures designed in Classical, Italianate, Renaissance and French Baroque styles.

Whilst the private textile warehouse was the most dramatic of the multi-storey industrial warehouses, the most influential design of the period was the single storey transit shed, which was to predomi-nate in the twentieth century. Such sheds had an ancient pedigree but their use as transhipment centres, rather than warehouses, in the industrial period can be traced to the canal/railway termini of the early nineteenth century. The sheds on the Peak Forest Canal at the Buxworth rail terminus are amongst the earliest surviving examples, but Potato Wharf in the Castlefield Basin was characterised by a series of long, open-sided, sheds which allowed vehicular traffic close to the quayside. The reliability of steam trains, and later steam ships, allowed faster patterns of distribution to emerge in the mid-nineteenth century, particularly on the dockside where the need for long-term storage was reduced by these speedier forms of transport. Increasingly there was a need for a quick and efficient means of transhipping goods and two types of transit shed were developed to answer this problem. Firstly, the open-sided shed with the dock on one side and the railway on the other. Such an arrangement was employed at Poplar Docks in London as early as the 1860s, whilst amongst the earliest surviving dock-side transit sheds are those from the West Princes Dock in Liverpool (Ashmore 1982, 161–3). Secondly, the enclosed shed with sliding doors to allow road and rail transport in and out. This was the design adopted for the Liverpool Shipping Warehouses in Trafford Park, although both types of transit shed were used in the facilities developed in the Pomona Docks, the Trafford Park industrial estate and at Dock 6 in the Salford Docks from the late 1890s onwards (Fig 1.7; McNeil 1997, 52). The introduction of the hydraulic crane, first patented in 1846, was also a significant contributor to the rapid bulk loading and unloading of goods in the later nineteenth century (Stratton and Trinder 1997, 96).

Fig 1.7 Trafford Park.
Trafford Park was the world's first purpose built industrial park. It was served by its own railway network and a range of multi-storey and single storey steel and concrete warehouses designed for road, rail and canal distribution. It is still an important commercial and retail distribution centre, although now largely by road. Photograph: Professor Barri Jones.

The Twentieth-century Storage Revolution

The twentieth century witnessed a change in the way in which goods were handled for redistribution. This was driven by the introduction of the motor-vehicle in the 1900s, containerisation in the 1950s and later by computer technology and led to the abandonment of multi-storey city-centre warehouses in favour of single-storey transit sheds located close to, or at, road junctions. The use of fork-lift trucks from the 1920s which could lift wooden pallets supporting all manner of goods coupled with conveyor belts produced a narrow, single storey, building plan without the need for raised floors. This reduced the distance between taking-in and dispatch, but allowed extra room to store different materials in different aisles. Inevitably this called for large hectares of space which often could only be supplied on out of town sites. The growing use of computers in the second half of the century allowed such structures to grow in area and height, whilst keeping a tight control on their contents (Stratton and Trinder 1997, 103–5). At the same time the concept of long term storage fell out of use, and the transhipment centre became the dominant form of store. With the collapse of Britain's canal system in the mid-twentieth century, both the Ashton and Peak Forest canals had been completely abandoned by 1960 for instance, and the drastic decline in goods taken by rail in the late twentieth century most of the old-style Victorian multi-storey warehouses fell out of use and ware-house design returned to a simpler form which the Romans might have recognised.

2

Portland Basin and the Canal Warehouse in North West England

Introduction

North West England was the site of Britain's first and last industrial canal warehouses. The Duke's Warehouse, arguably the first canal warehouse to have the classic design features of internal canal arms, multi-storeys, split level loading, terracing and water powered hoists, was built between 1769 and 1771. The Great Northern Warehouse was the last of the monumental road, rail and canal interchanges to be built in the Victorian period. Finished in 1898 it marked the end of the canal warehouse tradition and the beginning of motorised road transport storage. Between the two buildings, both in Manchester, were nearly 130 years of innovation and change. With at least 58 surviving canal warehouses across the region (see gazetteer), from Lancaster in the north to Bunbury in the south, the North West contains one of the largest, and most important, groups of canal warehouses in Europe. Their design influenced the building of the first railway warehouses, and later the cotton warehouse, and although the canals were superseded by the railways the canal warehouse remained an important element of the transport economy until the arrival of road haulage in the 1920s. The Portland Basin Warehouse (Fig 2.1) was built at the zenith of what became known as the Canal Age, in the 1830s, and, at 4,026m² in area, is amongst the largest examples to survive in the region. This chapter describes that warehouse and its archaeological context within the region.

The Portland Basin Canal Warehouse

The Ashton Canal Warehouse, it did not become known as the Portland Basin warehouse until the twentieth century, is one of at least 58 canal warehouses to survive in North West England. By the late nineteenth century there may have been as many as 100 canal warehouses in the region and these ranged in size from small ware-houses of a few hundred square metres in area, such as the example on Melbourne Street in Stalybridge, to the huge complex of the Great

Northern Warehouse which had a storage and transhipment floor area of 26,730m². Five canal warehouses are known to have been built in Tameside, of which four survive; Hyde Wharf on the Peak Forest Canal, Portland Basin on the Ashton Canal, Stalybridge Melbourne Street and Stalybridge Cornmill both on the Huddersfield Canal. By far the largest warehouse structure in Tameside, and one of the largest to survive in the region, is the Portland Basin, which in floor area compares with the largest examples built at Ellesmere Port, Liverpool and Manchester during the 1830s and 1840s. The original building was constructed by the firm of David Bellhouse & Co, who also built the 1830 Liverpool Road railway warehouse, in the years 1832–4 for the Ashton Canal Company at a cost of £8,901 13s. 3d. Two other canal warehouses had been built by the firm for the Ashton Canal Company at their Ducie Street Manchester terminus in 1798, at a cost of £1,000 and at the Heaton Norris Stockport terminus in 1799 for a similar cost (Keaveney and Brown 1974, 8). The family firm may also have been responsible for the design and building of the Ashton Old Wharf Warehouse. The foundations of this warehouse, and its two internal canal arms, which are still water filled, can be seen at the junction of the Ashton and Huddersfield Canals. The

Fig 2.1 The southern elevation of the Portland Basin Warehouse in the 1960s.
By this date the Ashton Canal was disused, although the warehouse continued in use as a storage for a road haulage firm.

Portland Basin Warehouse was the last, largest and most expensive of all the warehouses built for the Ashton Canal Company, and the only one still standing in anything like its original form.

The Portland Basin lies at the junction of the Ashton and Peak Forest Canals in the Portland Place area of Ashton-under-Lyne. Here a large U-shaped basin leads to the Portland Basin Warehouse, a building of classic canal warehouse design. This three storey building, built in English Garden Wall bond brick (four rows of brick laid end to end alternating with one row laid side-by-side) is 13 bays long and 5 bays deep, and terraced into the hillside on its northern elevation, where just two storeys rise above ground level.

The southern, canal facade has three storeys, with stone quoins to the doorways and stone lintels and sills to all of the openings. This impressive facade includes three central archways with stone rusticated surrounds, all of which allowed access for boats into the warehouse. Two further archways on either side of the wharf arm, also with stone rusticated surrounds, provided cart access into the building and above each of these were large rectangular taking-in doors each with its own crane. The wharf side of the warehouse is still enclosed by high, coped, brick walls and two pairs of cast-iron gates, to discourage theft and pilfering. Ground floor windows on the western, northern and eastern elevations also had iron bars to improve security. A separate jib crane lay on the eastern bank of the basin and was used

Fig 2.2 The western elevation of the Portland Basin Warehouse in the 1960s.
The drop in the ground level between the northern side (left) and southern canal side (right) of the warehouse is clearly visible in this view, as are two rectangular loading bays with a semi-circular cathead hoist cover above. Note the roof style with its coped gable and kneelers; the central five bays of the warehouse had a flat roof structure.

for unloading canal boats away from the warehouse. The two storey northern elevation had just 10 bays, because of the 45° angle of the short western and eastern walls which was a result of terracing the building into the hillside. Here there were five loading bays, each with two rectangular taking-in doors, one on top of the other, topped by external hoists and wooden cathead canopies (Figs 2.2 and 2.3). There was also a grand central entrance surrounded by stone quoins. Both the western and eastern walls each had five bays which included a single loading area with external hoists and cathead canopies three bays in from the southern canal side.

Internally the warehouse had three timber floors each supported by cast iron columns (Fig 2.4). Some of these columns, both within the main body of the building and alongside the internal canal arms, had brackets for hoist mechanisms, and examples of these hoists survive in the museum. Trap doors in the two floors above the internal canal arms allowed for internal split loading and unloading. Although of classic canal warehouse design the building has three unusual features. Firstly, it has three internal canal arms which ran

Fig 2.3 The northern elevation of the Portland Basin Warehouse in the 1960s.
The view shows the roadside loading area with its two storey rectangular loading bays with a semi-circular cathead hoist cover above. The chimneys behind the warehouse belong to the Junction Mill complex.

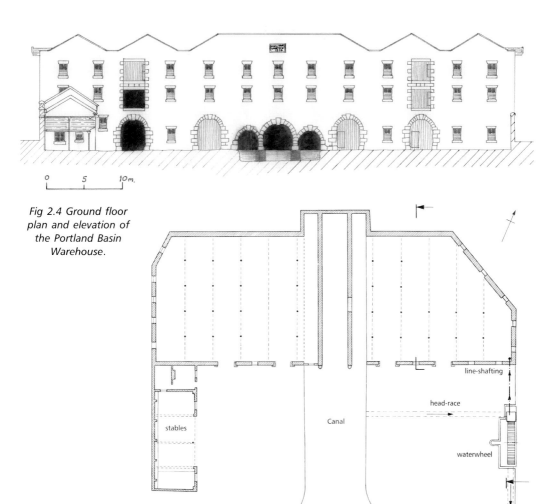

Fig 2.4 Ground floor plan and elevation of the Portland Basin Warehouse.

line-shafting

head-race

Canal

stables

waterwheel

0   10m

parallel to each other, each *c.* 25m long, the outer two arms *c.* 2.5m wide, the central arm *c.* 4.5m wide. In the 1820s and 1830s the usual design included just two internal canal arms, at least in the North West. The use of three canal arms allowed three canal boats to be unloaded at once, giving the warehouse an extra 50% internal loading capacity. Although divided by two brick walls, openings in these walls gave access to all three canal arms. Secondly, the roof structure of the warehouse was not the usual single span pitch roof, or even the rarer multi-pitched roof. Its design incorporated a long flat-roofed section which covered the central five bays, whilst the remaining eight bays, four to each side of the central section, were covered by two pairs of double pitched roof. None of the other surviving warehouses in the North West have this particular roof structure.

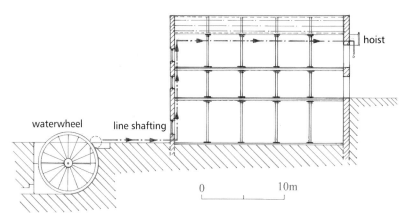

Fig 2.5 The relationship of the water wheel to Portland Basin. A cross-section showing how the power was transmitted from the water wheel to the internal hoist system within the Portland Basin warehouse.

The use of such a design must have been to increase the storage volume of the top floor. Thirdly, it had an external waterwheel fed from the canal, which powered the internal hoist system. This arrangement was not a primary feature (Fig 2.5). Originally, the cranes used for loading and unloading the goods in the warehouse were operated by hand, and fragments of this hoist system, including a jib crane and a wooden fly wheel can still be seen within the museum. This system was obviously felt to be inadequate and during the years 1839–41 a water-wheel was installed to provide additional lifting power for heavier and bulkier loads. Situated outside the south-eastern corner of the warehouse, in its own brick wheel house, it was fed from a headrace which left the northern bank of the canal wharf in front of the warehouse via a weir just outside the eastern boat hole. The flow of water was controlled by the penstock which was originally opened or closed from inside the warehouse. The water then drained away from the wheel pit exiting via a sloping tailrace into the northern bank of the River Tame, approximately 10m below the level of the canal (Owen 1977, 84–5).

The waterwheel, which was rebuilt in 1988 by Dorothea Restorations Ltd of Whaley Bridge in Derbyshire, is a high breast-shot suspension wheel made of cast and wrought iron (Fig 2.6). This type of waterwheel was introduced in 1811 by the Manchester millwright and engineer Thomas Hewes, and further developed by William Fairburn, who having worked for Thomas Hewes established a successful engineering business in Manchester. Such a design has three key features. Firstly, the suspension wheel replaced the pit wheel with gear teeth mounted on the rim or shroud of the wheel, known as rim gearing. Secondly, the drive shaft gear could rotate at greater speeds, which greatly enhanced mechanization by permitting power to be transmitted

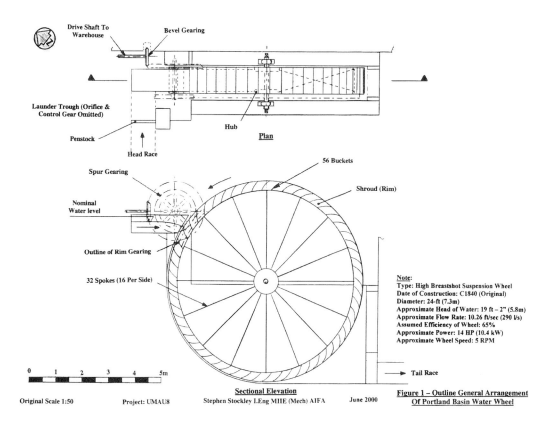

Drive Shaft To Warehouse

Bevel Gearing

Launder Trough (Orifice & Control Gear Omitted)

Hub

Plan

Penstock

Head Race

Spur Gearing

56 Buckets

Shroud (Rim)

Nominal Water level

Outline of Rim Gearing

32 Spokes (16 Per Side)

Note:
Type: High Breastshot Suspension Wheel
Date of Construction: C1840 (Original)
Diameter: 24-ft (7.3m)
Approximate Head of Water: 19 ft – 2" (5.8m)
Approximate Flow Rate: 10.26 ft/sec (290 l/s)
Assumed Efficiency of Wheel: 65%
Approximate Power: 14 HP (10.4 kW)
Approximate Wheel Speed: 5 RPM

0   1   2   3   4   5m

Tail Race

Sectional Elevation

Original Scale 1:50   Project: UMAU8   Stephen Stockley I.Eng MIIE (Mech) AIFA   June 2000

Figure 1 – Outline General Arrangement Of Portland Basin Water Wheel

Fig 2.6 The general arrangement of the Portland Basin water wheel.
Drawn by Steve Stockley.

at higher speeds and greater distances. Thirdly, the rim gearing reduced the strain on the axle and spokes, which allowed a lighter construction similar to a bicycle wheel.

The Portland Basin waterwheel cost £1,078 0s. 6½d. to build, produced nearly 15hp, and is 3ft ⅜" (0.92m) wide and 24 feet (7.3m) in diameter. The rim assembly has a depth of shroud of 13" (0.33m), which houses 56 non-ventilated buckets (Fig 2.7). The wheel rim is supported by 32 iron spokes, 16 on each side, which are bolted to two shaft mounted hubs of just over 36" (0.92m) diameter. These hubs are secured by wedges to a 6.18" (0.16m) diameter axle or shaft. The wheel assembly is mounted between two 'Plumber Block' type bearings bolted to stone sills that form part of the support structure and wheel pit. The wheel took its water from the canal basin to the west, where it flowed down a culverted headrace 22.7m in length. This culverted section had two penstocks, the first 1.8m from its entrance, the second 1m from the launder trough. From here the flow turned 90° into the launder trough and exited into the wheel pit via an adjustable opening, before being discharged into the River Tame. The rotary motion to the hoists (Fig 2.8) was transmitted

*Fig 2.7 The Remains
of the 1840s
waterwheel.*
The waterwheel was
installed in 1841 to
provide extra lifting
power for the heaviest
loads. Unusually, it
was located in a
detached wheel house,
seen here in a view
from the 1960s.
Equally unusual was
the water supply,
which came from a
leat running off the
Ashton Canal which
discharged into the
River Tame.

through a spur and bevel gear drive shaft system that is made from two sub-assemblies; a short drive shaft 1.33m long comprising pinion and bevel gear mounted at 90° to the centre line of the wheel, and a main drive shaft 9.5m long comprising bevel gears that run parallel to the centre line of the wheel. With a wheel speed of around 5 RPM, the short drive shaft would have rotated at around 25 RPM and the main drive shaft at 42 RPM. The drive shaft entered the warehouse at its south-eastern corner and once inside the mill the power was transmitted by a vertical shaft to each floor, from where horizontal line shafting and gears powered the hoists which were independently controlled on each floor.

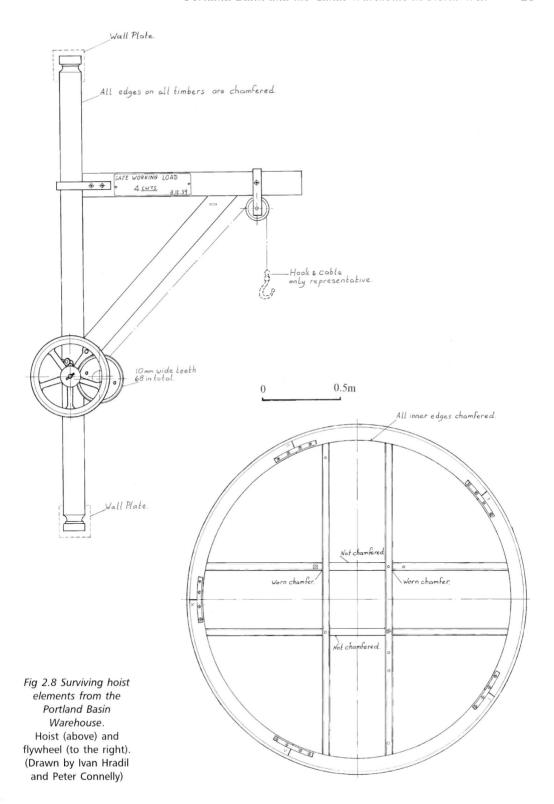

Wall Plate.

All edges on all timbers are chamfered.

SAFE WORKING LOAD
4 CWTS   8.12.39

Hook & cable
only representative.

10 mm wide teeth
68 in total.

0   0.5m

Wall Plate.

All inner edges chamfered.

Not chamfered

Worn chamfer.   Worn chamfer.

Not chamfered.

Fig 2.8 Surviving hoist elements from the Portland Basin Warehouse.
Hoist (above) and flywheel (to the right).
(Drawn by Ivan Hradil and Peter Connelly)

The Origin of the Classic Canal Warehouse

As an archaeological monument type the canal warehouse was a product of the Industrial Revolution and was one of a number of industrial warehouse types that developed from 1760 onwards (RCHME 1996). Although it owed much to its coastal and urban predecessors, in its most developed form the canal warehouse was an innovative structure combining multi-storeys, split level loading, terracing, internal water-filled canal arms and a hoist system run by water power. This unique form appears to have been developed in North West England during the 1760s and 1770s.

It is relatively easy to find antecedents for three of the five major elements of the classic canal warehouse design. Multi-storeyed warehouses had long been in use in urban contexts and during the early and mid-eighteenth century many dock facilities around Britain, from Lancaster to London, were being rebuilt using just such buildings (Crowe 1994, 65–7). These structures often used split level loading via external man- or horse-powered hoists attached to the top of the waterside elevation of the structure. In the North West the Mersey and Irwell Navigation Co. was amongst the first to build such structures during the redevelopment of their Manchester and Warrington quays in the 1720s and 1730s (Hadfield and Biddle 1971). One of these structures in particular may have provided the inspiration for the classic canal warehouse design. The Rock House was erected by the Mersey and Irwell Navigation Co. in Manchester by 1728. It lay on the eastern bank of the River Irwell, just south of the site of the present Blackfriars Bridge in the area of the Parsonage, where it is shown on S & N Buck's view of the south-western prospect of the town from that year. This building was located on the edge of a sheer cliff above the river, a drop of roughly 15m. In order to over come the height difference between the two a four-storey split level loading warehouse was built flush with the river bank but terraced into the hillside. The river facade had an external hoist system and four storeys, whilst the road side had just two storeys, allowing boats to be unloaded via a jib crane directly into carts at road level (Tomlinson 1961, 130–1).

Yet it was the two final elements of the canal warehouse, the internal water-filled canal arms that brought the canal right into the centre of the structure and a hoist system run by water power, combined with the multi-storey dock and urban warehouse with its split level loading tradition, that made the building type revolutionary. The development of such a bold building may have been as much an accident of geography as the result of industrial inspiration. The topography of the River Medlock through the Castlefield area of Manchester was very similar to that of the Irwell below Manchester Cathedral, with sheer cliffs at a number of points along the river valley between the line of Deansgate and the junction of the River Medlock with the River Irwell. In 1763 Castlefield was chosen by James Brindley as the terminus for the Duke of Bridgewater's new industrial canal that would bring coal from his mines at Worsley Delph into the heart of Manchester. Clearly the height difference between the river and the town, approximately 7.7m (25ft) would be a problem when unloading the coal from the Duke's mines. The Castlefield basin of the Bridgewater Canal was opened in the summer of 1765 (Malet 1977, 99; Tomlinson 1961, 132–3) but lacked any warehouse facilities so initially coals were hauled by carts up a steep routeway cut into the northern terrace of the River Medlock. By 1769 a number of cottages had been converted into warehouses on the northern bank of the River Medlock where it was crossed by the line of Deansgate; these are shown on Young's map of the Castlefield Basin published in 1770 (Tomlinson 1961, 139–40). As Tomlinson has detailed, Young's contemporary description of the canal basin shows that Brindley had something more ambitious in mind as a way of overcoming the 7.7m height difference between river and town. No doubt using the experience he had gained in building the underground network of canals at the Worsley coal mines (Aldred 1988; Boucher 1968; Malet 1977), Brindley built a brick-arched tunnel that ran from the northern side of the Medlock northwards below the line of the modern Castle Street, from which level a shaft was sunk and a swivel crane used to haul 8cwt boxes of coal directly from the canal boats to the roadway. Power was provide by a 30ft diameter waterwheel which turned a wooden cylinder carrying a rope for operating the crane, whilst a sluice controlled a flow of water from the underground canal so that it passed through a rock-cut channel to drive the waterwheel (Tomlinson 1961, 140). Here, then, were the two missing elements of the classic canal warehouse design, the covered canal arm and the water-powered hoist system. The great leap of linking these and the split level dock warehouse in one structure must have been made by James Brindley himself.

Thus was born the canal warehouse with its distinctive shipping holes, water-powered hoist system, split level loading, multi-storeys and terraced location that quickly became the hallmark of this type of warehouse. However, it is not clear which of the Castlefield buildings was the first true industrial canal warehouse. Tomlinson demonstrated as long ago as 1961 that the five storey brick Grocer's Warehouse was built over Brindley's 1760s canal tunnel, and re-used

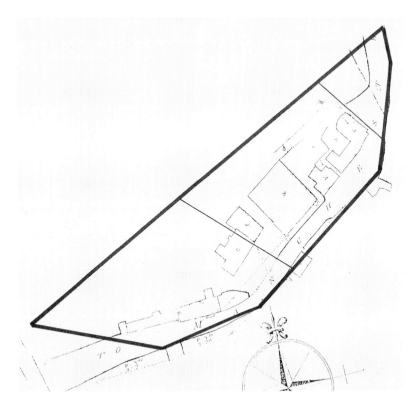

Fig 2.9 Plans of the Duke's Warehouse "B", in Castlefield, Manchester in 1771 (left) and 1794 (right). This was almost certainly the first classic canal warehouse, with split level loading and internal canal arms, to be built in Britain. Taken from the Bridgewater Archives and William Green's survey of Manchester and Salford. Reproduced by permission of Salford Libraries.

this structure in its own design, producing internally a skewed 80° canal arm which is probably unique in canal architecture (Tomlinson 1961, 140–2). The date of this warehouse, judging from the map evidence, lies in the period 1770–78. Circumstantial evidence led Tomlinson to believe that the first purpose built canal warehouse of this classic design was the nearby Duke's Warehouse (so-called because it was built for the Duke of Bridgewater as part of his canal works), which straddled the River Medlock at the head of the canal basin, just east of the modern Deansgate Bridge. However, he lacked the detailed evidence to prove that this five storey brick warehouse with its two internal canal arms was built before the late 1770s. During documentary research prior to the excavation of the remains of the Duke's warehouse in 1998 a map of the Deansgate area around the River Medlock was re-discovered in the Bridgewater archives. Dating from 1771 the map shows a rectangular building (site B) straddling the Medlock and describes this as the 'new warehouse', proving that the Duke's was the first canal warehouse and suggesting that it was designed by Brindley himself (Fig 2.9).

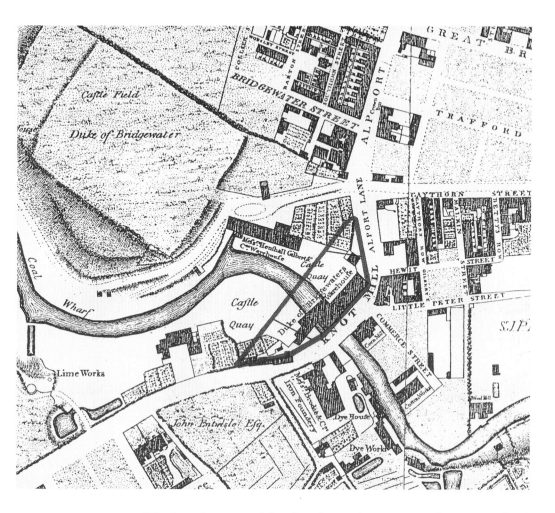

The Development of the Canal Warehouse in North West England

The Portland Basin is one of at least 58 surviving canal warehouses
in North West England. A rapid survey of these surviving buildings
for the present study indicates that there was a wide range of architectural styles and plan forms along the canals of the region, though
each canal company appears to have had its own style. The Bridgewater Canal favoured classically inspired buildings with pediments
and circular windows. While the Shropshire Union Canal appears to
have preferred buildings constructed in the vernacular tradition, in
local styles and local materials. In contrast the Ashton and Rochdale
Canal companies favoured large, austere warehouses reminiscent of
the functional restrained polite style of local textile mill designs
during the early nineteenth century. Their wide date range (1770 to
1898) masks the fact that most of the warehouses were built in a

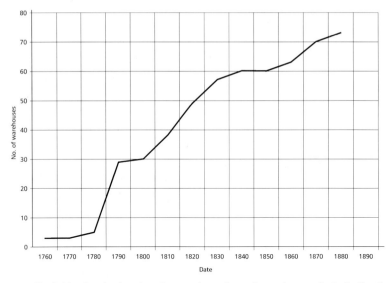

Fig 2.10a Graph showing the number of canal warehouses built in North West England during the years 1770 to 1900.

forty year period between 1800 and 1840 (see Fig 2.10). Furthermore, when viewed as a single group, it becomes clear that the major variations in design stem from their plan form, although the increasing use of new buildings materials was also a significant factor in their development.

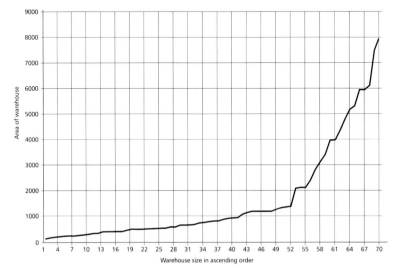

Fig 2.10b Graph showing the size of the canal warehouses built in North West England.

The Type 1 Warehouse

Across the region four major plan forms have been identified in the surviving canal warehouses (Fig 2.11). The earliest and most important plan form (Type 1) was the classic canal warehouse plan with its internal canal arm. Surviving examples in North West England span the period 1770 to 1898. The earliest examples, the Duke's and Grocers' Warehouses, appear to have been designed by James Brindley for the Bridgewater Canal's Castlefield basin in the early 1770s. How quickly this design spread along the burgeoning canal network of Britain is unclear, but in 1777 the terminal warehouse in Wigan was built by the Leeds and Liverpool Canal, by the late 1770s Sir John Ramsden's Aspley Warehouse had been built on the Huddersfield Broad Canal

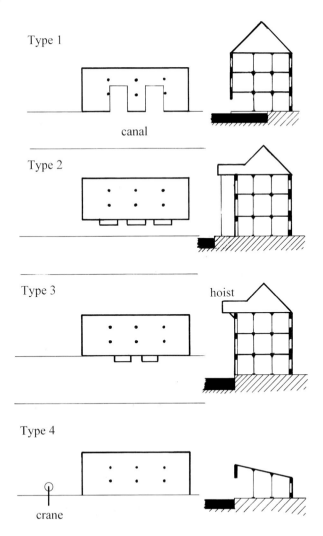

Fig 2.11 Schematic plans of the four main types of canal warehouse in North West England.

and by 1780 this design was being used at the canal town of Shardlow on the Trent and Mersey Canal in a small warehouse built with a classical pediment and datestone above the segmental-arched boat hole. Like Aspley's this was a largely plain building in the restrained classical or "polite" style typical of many early industrial structures (Crowe 1994, 73). By 1800 canal warehouses of this type were being designed for waterways as far apart as the Calder and Hebble Navigation in Yorkshire and the Coventry Canal (Crowe 1994, 80). The usefulness of this classic design is shown by its adoption over the next forty years in many of the great cities of the Industrial Revolution; Birmingham, Glasgow, Leeds, Liverpool, London, Manchester and Sheffield.

In the North West the further spread of the warehouse with its internal canal arm had to await the canal boom of the 1790s and many of the surviving examples in the region belong to the first decades of the nineteenth century when the support infrastructure for these new waterways was being completed. The warehouses at Ashton Old Wharf, Bury, Chester, Kendal, Liverpool, Marple, Stockport and Wigan all fall into this date range and were characterised by single internal canal arm warehouses (Fig 2.12). Amongst this group is an interesting variant, where the canal arm, instead of running at 90° from the canal side, runs parallel to it, probably because of the pressure on canal side space. Good examples of this variant can still be seen on the Peak Forest Canal in Marple where the fine stone warehouse was built by Samuel Oldknow around *c.* 1801–5 and the later 1830s warehouse on the Macclesfield Canal in the same town. The Bury wharf canal warehouse of *c.* 1810, demolished in the 1960s, was a striking three storey brick building where the canal ran the full length of the building exiting through the northern gable before continuing to a private coal wharf. A fine surviving example of this kind of warehouse can still be seen at Worksop on the Chesterfield Canal (Crowe 1994, 79). The most elegant of this variant on the classic design is Telford's Chester Warehouse built alongside the Chester Canal basin around 1830.

The peak in the design of the Type 1 canal warehouse was reached in the 1820s and 1830s when a series of fine double and even triple internal canal arm warehouses were built across the region. In Manchester this particular form of the Type 1 warehouse became characteristic not only of the Bridgewater but also the Ashton and Rochdale canal basins. In the Castlefield basin a massive building programme saw the construction of five Warehouses between 1827 (The Merchant's) and *c.* 1840 (Kenworthy, Fig 2.13), each larger than the previous one and as a grouping they remained the biggest canal

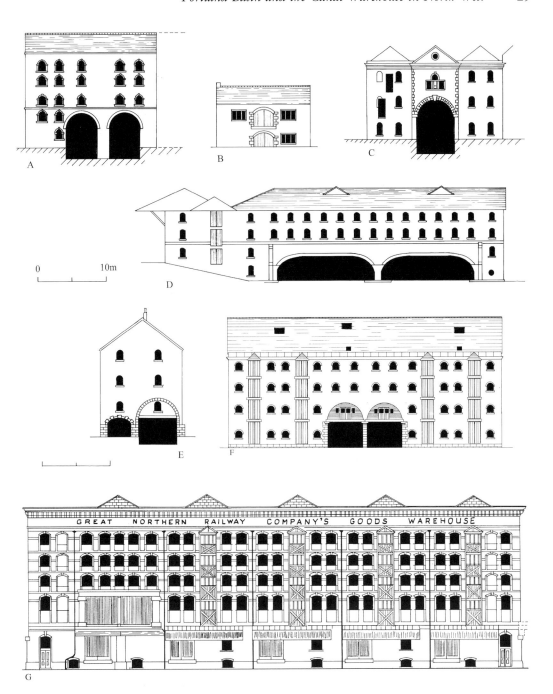

Fig 2.12 Canalside warehouse elevations from around North West England.
A The Grocers' Warehouse, Bridgewater Canal, Castelfield; B Foulridge Warehouse, Leeds and Liverpool Canal; C Broadheath Warehouse, Bridgewater Canal; D Telford's Winged Warehouse, Ellesmere Port, Shropshire, Chester and Ellesmere Canal; E Bury Terminal Warehouse, Manchester, Bolton and Bury Canal; F Merchant's Warehouse, Bridgewater Canal, Castelfield; G Great Northern Warehouse, Manchester and Salford Junction Canal, Manchester.

warehouses in the region. Despite their size the two warehouses that stand out from this period are the Portland Basin and Telford's winged warehouse at Ellesmere Port. Although both were largely destroyed by fire in the early 1970s the Portland Basin warehouse has been recently rebuilt, and once more the three unusual features of its design (the flat roof, three internal canal arms and external water-wheel powered by the canal) can be admired. The pinnacle of the Type 1 canal warehouse was undoubtedly Telford's winged warehouse at Ellesmere. Completed in 1835 this E-shaped building had four storeys built between the upper and lower canal basins at Ellesmere Port. Cargoes were unloaded in the lower basin from boats which could sail under three arches, each over 13m in width, carted through the building and then out in to the upper basin, which was roughly 5m higher than the lower basin, where the cart loading area was protect by a large timber awning (Crowe 1994; Roberts 1995). These were the largest arched shipping hole spans in the region and dwarfed the 9m spans seen in the largest of the Manchester warehouses.

After 1840, the competition from the new railway companies led to most of the canals in the region being taken over by them. Consequently, new transport warehouse building concentrated on the railways in the later nineteenth century. The last pure Type 1 canal warehouse was built at Ellesmere Port in 1871. The Grain Warehouse, as it was known, still stands today (Fig 2.14). A large two storey multi-roof structure of cast-iron, 30.5m × 51.6m in plan, the internal canal arm running the full length of the western side of the building, the 10m span of the internal canal arm carried on wrought iron

Fig 2.13 Kenworthy Warehouse, Castlefield. This nineteenth-century view shows canal boats unloading in the classic internal canal arms which characterised the Type 1 Canal Warehouse.

Fig 2.14 Island Grain Warehouse, Ellesmere Port.
Built in 1871 this was the last of the classic Type 1 Warehouses to built in North West England. The opening for the internal canal arm can be seen in the middle of the picture.

girders. The railway/canal interchanges of the late nineteenth century subsumed the classic canal warehouse design and it is perhaps fitting that the grandest of these Victorian railway masterpieces, the steel framed Great North Warehouse, was opened in Manchester in 1898 (Stratton and Trinder 1997, 98–9). The dominance of the railway by this date was complete and although the Manchester and Salford Junction Canal runs across the full width of the building it is completely hidden from view in the basement of the five storey structure.

The Type 2 Warehouse

The next major form of canal warehouse in the region was the warehouse which was detached from canal side (Type 2). This was the most common type of canal warehouse in the North West and surviving examples in the region span the period 1790 to 1890. Essentially these were traditional multi-storey warehouses which were built by the side of the canal, and across Britain a number of warehouses of this type can still be seen in the canal towns such as Goole, Shardlow and Stourport (Crowe 1994, 69–73; Smith 1997). In the North West surviving examples include buildings from Chester, Church Lawton, Dugdale, Finsley, Foulridge, High Lane, Leigh,

Liverpool, Manchester Water Street, Middlewich, Sandbach and Wigan. They were particularly popular along the Shropshire Union and Leeds and Liverpool canal companies. Since this form of canal warehouse relied on a separate jib crane by the canal side for loading and unloading they were unsuitable for most urban locations where the volume of traffic demanded more flexible designs. The progression in canal warehouse design can be seen particularly well at Burnley and Blackburn where Type 2 warehouses built around 1800 were supplemented by the more versatile Type 4 warehouses in the mid- and late nineteenth century.

In the mid-nineteenth century the introduction of a projecting hoist tower provided the Type 2 warehouse with a new lease of life. Whilst the warehouse remained set back from the canal side a multi-storey hoist tower projected over the canal side allowing boats to be unload and loaded directly into the warehouse. The mid-nineteenth-century warehouse at Preston Brook Wharf on the Trent and Mersey Canal is an early regional example of this approach, but the projecting hoist tower became a feature of the Leeds and Liverpool Canal wharfs in Burnley, Blackburn, Nelson and Wigan in the later nineteenth century (Fig 2.15).

The small-scale nature of the Type 2 warehouse (they were usually less than 1,000m^2 in floor area) appears to have been well suited to rural trade and the Shropshire Union Canal continued to build such warehouses down to the end of the nineteenth century, good examples still surviving at Bunbury, Church Lawton, Sandbach and Middlewich.

Fig 2.15 A Wigan Canal Warehouse. This Type 2 building was erected in the 1880s and is part of a regionally important grouping of three warehouses. It is typical of the canal warehouses built by the Leeds and Liverpool Canal Company in this period, with its vernacular detailing and multi-storey hoist tower.

The Type 3 Warehouse

Contemporary with the Type 2 warehouse, but generally much larger in construction, was the multi-storey warehouse running parallel but flush to the canal side (Type 3). This allowed for direct loading and unloading from canal boats usually via cathead cranes on the canal side of the building and avoided the expense of building internal canal arms. A variation to this was the use of a jib crane built into the corner of the warehouse. A fine example of the use of this technique survives at Dugdale Wharf in Burnley which dates to about 1800. The economy of space the design provided may explain why it was the second most common form of canal warehouse in the region. The surviving examples across the North West in Burnley, Congleton, Hest Bank, Heatley, Hyde, Lancaster, Liverpool, Leigh, Preston and Stalybridge span the 1800s to the 1890s, but elsewhere in Britain this design has a much longer span (Crowe 1994, 76). Dockside buildings in Portsmouth and London had been built flush with the waterside earlier in the eighteenth century (Stratton and Trinder 1997, 91–2) whilst steel framed examples of this type of building, with awnings projecting over the canal side, were built as late as the 1960s at Apsley and Brentford on the Grand Union Canal (Crowe 1994, 76–7). The most impressive surviving grouping of Type 2 warehouses can be found in the Gloucester Docks where five, six, seven and eight storey brick warehouses built between 1826 and 1873 still line the waterside (Crowe 1994, 69; Smith 1996, 25). A number of the dockside warehouses at Trafford Park in Manchester and Salford Quays followed in this tradition during the early twentieth century.

The Type 4 Warehouse

The open sided shed, built flush with the canal side, appears to have been a late introduction into the canal architecture of North West England. This was despite its long history as a dockside building type. Examples in the region do not survive before 1840 (it is not clear if any examples of this type were built before that date) and were still being constructed in the 1890s. This type of large shed was favoured by the Leeds and Liverpool Canal Company, examples surviving from their wharfs in Blackburn, Burnley, Nelson and Wigan (Clarke 1990, 101–2 and 196–200). The introduction of wrought iron framing from the 1840s onwards allowed the construction of these tall, single storey, buildings with hoists in a roof which was often projected over the canal side. Given the building type's history as a dock structure it is perhaps unsurprising that it was used by the

Mersey and Irwell Navigation Company at their Warrington wharf and remained a feature of dock architecture into the twentieth century (McNeil 1997).

Warehouse Design and the Introduction of New Building Materials

A brief review of the floor area of the canal warehouse in North West England indicates that they ranged in size from the tiny warehouse at Clayton Bridge in Lancaster (if that is what the original function of the building was) at 102m^2 to the monumental Great Northern Warehouse at 26,730m^2. The difference between these buildings is not just their size, it is also their style and form of construction.

The earliest canal warehouses of the late eighteenth century were often single bay-depth brick or stone structures of one or two storeys. Surviving examples of this include warehouses at Shardlow and Stourport (Crowe 1994, 72–3) and this type of warehouse continued to be built throughout the nineteenth century. The floors were wooden and because the width of these buildings did not exceed 7m there was rarely a need to support the floors with timber or cast-iron posts. Buildings such as the small two storey, stone Type 2 warehouse at Foulridge built around 1800 on the Leeds and Liverpool Canal or the two storey, stone Type 3 warehouse at Hest Bank built around 1820 on the Lancaster Canal were constructed in the local vernacular tradition with mullioned windows, quoining and wide cart entrances reminiscent of local threshing barns. Similar single span two or three storey vernacular warehouses survive along the Shropshire Union Canal at Bunbury Locks and on the Trent and Mersey Canal at Church Lawton, Middlewich and Sandbach in date spanning the whole of the nineteenth century.

The single bay-depth warehouse built in the local vernacular style was unable to cope with the high volume of canal traffic required in the rapidly growing industrial towns of the region. Here the classic canal warehouse was developed with its internal canal arms. This kind of structure required a multiple depth building and in the late-eighteenth and early-nineteenth centuries this took the form of a brick, sometimes stone, building two or three bays deep with wooden floors supported by timber posts. The Duke's Warehouse, built in the period 1769–71, used a brick spine wall that ran the length of the building to add support to the wide structure, but this feature does not appear to have been used elsewhere in the region. Brick cross-walls were used to help brace the multiple depth warehouse in some structures, most notably the Duke's and Oldknow's

Type 1 warehouses in Manchester and in later Type 2 warehouses in Blackburn and Burnley. The disadvantage of such walls was that they reduced the internal floor area.

The use of cast-iron columns to support timber beams and timber or stone floors was one way in the early nineteenth century that the floor area of the canal warehouses could be maximized. In the North West examples of this style of construction can still be seen at Dugdale dating from around 1800, Dale Street (Fig 2.16) and Tariff Street in Manchester (built in 1806 and 1836 respectively), and Portland Basin in Ashton-under-Lyne, built in 1834. The most daring of all canal warehouses, Telford's great winged warehouse at Ellesmere Port, which was finished in 1835, also used this design.

The use of cast-iron framing in canal warehouse construction across the region was rare. Despite that fact that the first building of this type was the Ditherington Flax Mill in Shrewsbury erected in 1796–7 (Stratton and Trinder 1997, 65) it was not until 1811 that a canal warehouse was built using this form of construction. This building, the Grain Warehouse at the Duke's Dock in Liverpool, had a floor area that was only exceeded by the Ellesmere Port and Manchester canal warehouses of the 1820s and 1830s. It was a striking, six storey, brick and stone structure that had a symmetrical elevation divided into ten bays, with the central two bays supporting a classical pediment and containing a pair of semi-circular boat holes set within a larger semi-circle (Crowe 1994, 66). Although the warehouse has been demolished this Palladian inspired design was used again in the Middle Warehouse built at Castlefield in 1831, although the cast-iron framing technique was not.

Fig 2.16 The Dale Street Warehouse. Built in 1806 by the Rochdale Canal Company this Type 1 canal warehouse contains the earliest surviving water-powered hoist system in the region.

In 1871 the two storey multiple span Grain Warehouse, at Ellesmere Port, was built using wrought-iron framing and cargoes were lifted directly from the boats by hydraulic cranes. The Type 4 single storey warehouses built by the Leeds and Liverpool Canal in the late nineteenth century at Blackburn, Burnley and Wigan all used wrought-iron framing in their construction. The ultimate canal warehouse in the region was the Great Northern Railway Company's Warehouse on Deansgate, Manchester, a huge structure covering 26,730m² built around a steel frame. Constructed in the period 1896–8 it marked the end of 120 years of canal warehouse design and the pinnacle of the Victorian railway warehouse (Stratton and Trinder 1997, 98).

The Great North Warehouse was designed by the engineer W X Foxlee, who created a multi-level rail, road and canal terminus, the first and second storeys being in effect two separate goods stations each served on its southern side by the two-tier railway yards. This design was not new, it had been used in a number of railway and canal warehouses in London such as the Great Northern Railway's Camden Lock transhipment house on the Regent's Canal (Crowe 1994, 75), but in the Great Northern it was taken to its limits. Wagons could either run down to the lower first storey of the building where they were shunted by hydraulic capstans or be moved between the first and second storey by hydraulic lifts. Hoists provided a connection with the Manchester and Salford Junction Canal, which ran across the full length of the building at basement level. Carts, and later lorries, were loaded under cover, with a ramp giving then access to the second storey. This flexibility was made possible because the Great Northern was one of the first large steel-framed buildings in the country (Stratton and Trinder 1997, 98–9) and allowed very wide spans to be achieved without compromising the strength of the structure. An added benefit was that this material was perfect for fireproofing. Such innovation did not extend to the roof structure, which was timber.

Externally, the warehouse had more in common with contemporary mill design than the traditional polite architecture of the earlier canal warehouses. Designed in the Italianate style which Manchester had made its own in the late nineteenth century its red and blue walls were surmounted at cornice level by huge letters proclaiming the ownership of the site (George 1997, 38).

Storing the Past for the Future

Warehouses of all sorts remain a dominant part of the urban scene in North West England. However, the arrival of motorised road transport in the 1920s, and in the second half of the twentieth century the shift towards just-in-time working, has changed the nature of warehousing, making most of the canal warehouses of the region redundant. The growing demand for waterside apartments, offices and studios combined with the availability of grants in the 1990s has led to much conversion, restoration and new uses far removed from canal transhipment. Yet whilst the future of many canal warehouses is assured such new uses inevitably come at a cost and in most cases re-use has involved the loss of the large open plan internal spaces that characterised the canal warehouse. The Portland Basin warehouse is thus one of the few examples in the region where the public can still see all the features that created the classic canal warehouse design.

3

Portland Basin and the Ashton, Huddersfield and Peak Forest Canals

Introduction

Buildings such as Portland Basin were an integral part of one of the great transport networks of the Industrial Age; the canal. By 1830 there were over 4,000 miles of canal and river navigations in Britain carrying 30 million tonnes of goods each year. Over 550 miles of this network could be found in North West England, from Carlisle to Middlewich. This network encompassed 18 canals and 12 branches ranging in length from the Manchester and Salford Junction Canal at ⅝ of a mile to the Leeds and Liverpool Canal, at 127¼ miles the country's longest artificial waterway (Table 1), although only half of that lay in the North West.

The Birth of the Canal

Prior to industrialisation water transport, by both river and sea, was cheaper and quicker than using the unreliable road system (Armstrong 1989, 96). Even with the rise of the Turnpike Trust in the early eighteenth century the transportation of bulk loads by cart and pack horse was slow and expensive (Cootes 1982, 93). The Midlands pottery manufacturer Josiah Wedgwood, who campaigned for the building of the Trent and Mersey Canal in the 1760s, was reported as having been satisfied if one third of his delivery reached its destination in tact by road (Hadfield and Boughey 1998, 38–9). An answer to these problems was provided by the development of an artificial inland water system and the canals and their warehouses developed as a way of meeting this need for a more efficient and economic means of transporting bulk loads of goods, in particular coal for the newly developed steam engines, across the country. Yet the Georgians were not the first to build artificial waterways in Britain. The Romans had built an extensive network of canals around the Fenlands in eastern England, but these did not have the locks of their eighteenth-century

Table 1: The Canals and River Navigations of North West England

Canal	Construction period	Distance in miles	No of locks	Start/Finish
Ashton	1792–6	6¾	18	Manchester–Ashton
Ashton/Stockport Branch	1793–7	4⅞	0	Fairfield–Stockport
Ashton/Hollinwood Branch	1793–6	4⅝	7	Ashton–Hollinwood
Ashton/Fairbottom Branch	1793–7	1⅛	0	Ashton–Park Bridge
Bridgewater	1759–76	30¾	0	Worsley–Runcorn
Bridgewater/Leigh Branch	1795–1820	10¾	0	Worsley–Leigh
Bridgewater/Runcorn and Weston Branch	1853–9	1¼	2	Runcorn–Weston
Carlisle	1819–23	11¼	8	Carlisle–Port Carlisle
Huddersfield Narrow	1794–1811	19⅞	74	Huddersfield–Ashton
Lancaster	1792–1819	67¼	8	Westhoughton–Kendall
Lancaster/Glasson Branch	1792–1825	2½	6	Glasson–Galgate
Leeds and Liverpool	1770–1816	127¼	92	Leeds–Liverpool
Leeds and Liverpool/Rufford Branch	1777–81	7¼	8	Burscough–Tarleton
Leeds and Liverpool/Leigh Branch	1818–20	7¼	2	Wigan–Leigh
Macclesfield	1826–31	26⅛	13	Hardings Wood Junction–Marple Junction
Manchester, Bolton and Bury	1791–1808	11	17	Manchester–Bolton
Manchester, Bolton and Bury/Bury Branch	1791–6	4¾	0	Prestolee–Bury
Manchester and Salford Junction	1836–9	⅝	4	R. Irwell–Rochdale Canal (Mcr)
Manchester Ship Canal	1885–94	36	5	Salford Docks–Runcorn
Mersey and Irwell Navigation	1721–36	28¾	11	Manchester–Warrington
Mersey and Irwell Navigation/Runcorn	1799–1804	7¾	2	Runcorn–Latchford
Peak Forest	1794–1804	14¾	16	Whaley Bridge–Ashton
Rochdale	1794–1804	33	92	Sowerby Bridge–Manchester
St Helens (Sankey)	1755–57	8	10	Sankey Bridge–St Helens
St Helens/Widnes Branch	1830–33	3⅜	1	Widnes–Sankey Bridge
Shropshire Union (Chester and Ellesmere)	1772–1835	66½	47	Autherley Junction–Ellesmere
Shropshire Union/Middlewich Branch	1825–1833	10	4	Middlewich–Barbridge Junction
Trent and Mersey	1766–77	93½	76	Derwent Mouth–Preston Brook
Ulverston	1793	1½	1	R. Leven–Ulverston
Weaver Navigation	1721–32	18⅜	11	Winsford Bridge–Weston Point
Weaver Navigation/Weston Branch	1807–10	4	3	Frodsham Lock–Weston

Source: Hadfield 1966, Appendix 1; Hadfield and Biddle 1970, Appendix 1.

descendants. The French had built canals with locks in the seventeenth century. The most famous of these was the Canal du Midi built between 1666 and 1681 under the patronage of the King Louis XIV. It ran from the port of Sete on the Mediterranean coast to Toulouse where it joined the River Garonne (Clarke 1999, 27; Ransom 1979, 12–13). At 149 miles long with 101 locks lifting the canal to 620 feet above sea level there was nothing in Britain to rival it until the 1790s.

In Britain the late-seventeenth and early-eighteenth centuries were marked by developments in river navigations, where artificial cuts, often using locks, were used to shorten meandering rivers such as the Exe, in the 1670s; the Aire, Calder and Derwent in the 1700s; the Bristol Avon and Kennet in the 1710s; and, in North West England, the Douglas, Mersey and Weaver in the 1720s (Ransom 1979, 13). By the mid-eighteenth century all the technical elements existed to build an artificial waterway that was not a canalised river using techniques pioneered in continental Europe – in particular the concept of the lock which allowed canals to traverse hillsides via a series of tanks which could be filled with water by carefully controlling sluice gates whilst barges were inside the tank (Clarke 1999, 27–8; Hadfield and Biddle 1970, 15–16). These can all be seen in the eight miles of the Sankey Canal, later the St Helens Canal, authorised in 1755 and opened in 1757, although this was still essentially a river-based scheme (Hadfield and Boughey 1998, 15). What was needed was a grand project that would demonstrate the full potential of such a system, independent of the existing river waterways.

The catalyst which showed the value of the artificial waterway as a means of cheap, reliable, transport for bulk goods, was the construction of the Bridgewater Canal (Fig 3.1; Hadfield and Boughey 1998, 15–17). This was built by James Brindley for the third Duke of Bridgewater in the years 1759–76, initially to carry coal from the Duke's collieries in Worsley to Manchester, later extended to Runcorn and the Mersey estuary (Fig 3.2; Hadfield and Biddle 1970, 19–27). An Act of Parliament was needed to authorise the canal, and this was passed in 1759. By 1763 the Bridgewater Canal was opened as far as Stretford and by 1765 to Manchester. Its water supply came from the drainage of the colliery workinngs through an extensive underground canal system (Malet 1977, 97–9).

The success of the Bridgewater Canal led in the 1760s and 1770s to a phase described by Nigel Crowe as the era of the pioneering canals (Crowe 1994, 20–1). These early canals were characterised by contour and earth hugging artificial waterways with sinuous courses, large numbers of locks, few tunnels and few engineering risks. In the North West the only canals built during this era, besides the Bridgewater, were the Trent and Mersey, begun in 1766, the Leeds and Liver-

Fig 3.1 The Duke of Bridgewater. The Duke of Bridgewater demonstrates the engineering achievement of his canal at Barton where it was carried over the River Mersey in a stone aqueduct. The 'pioneering' canal era began with the building of the Bridgewater Canal. It was designed by James Brindley for the third Duke of Bridgewater in the years 1759–76 to carry coal from the Duke's collieries in Worsley to Manchester, but was later extended to Runcorn and the Mersey estuary.

Wigan Terminal Warehouse.

Burscough Wharf.

A reconstruction of the Portland Basin
Warehouse in Ashton-under-Lyne, as it
might have looked during the 1840s.
(*Drawn and painted by Graham Sumner*)

Above Tarleton Wharf.

Left Water wheel at Portland Basin.

pool, begun in 1770 and the Chester and Ellesmere in 1772 (Fig 3.3; Hadfield and Biddle 1970, 52). Whilst the Bridgewater was unique in being owned by one man, its private funding arrangements were copied by all subsequent canals. These pioneering canals were dominated by the local landowners and industrialists in their promotion; besides owning the Bridgewater Canal the Duke of Bridgewater helped promote and held shares in the Trent and Mersey Canal. His friend and brother-in-law Lord Gower, a Midlands landowner with extensive coal deposits on his land, was a leading promoter of the Trent and Mersey; whilst the Chester Canal was promoted by the leading citizens of Chester and financed by Lord Egerton (Hadfield 1969, 26–7; 166–7; Herson 1996, 77–8; Malet 1977, 105–11; Ward 1974). The background of the backers of the Leeds and Liverpool Canal foreshadowed the diversity of shareholders typical of the period 1790 to 1820, being promoted by a mixture of local landowners and the merchant classes of Liverpool and Leeds; but large land owners such as the Earl of Derby and the Bradshaighs, who both held extensive lands in Lancashire coalfields, were keen advocates if only out of self interest, whilst one of the canal's chief promoters was John Stanhope a Bradford landowner and attorney (Clarke 1990, 45, 48, 56–9).

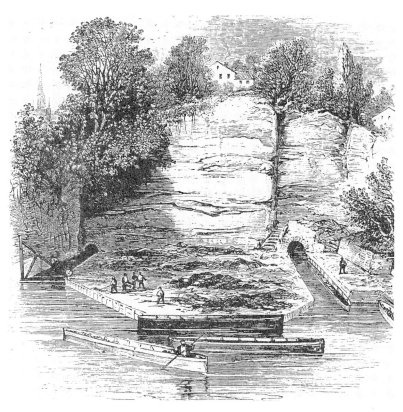

Fig 3.2 The Duke of Bridgewater's Canal works at Worsley. A late eighteenth-century view of the entrances to the underground canals at Worsley which served the Duke's coal mines there. These under ground canal tunnels were designed by James Brindley, the creator of the classic canal warehouse with internal canal arms and internal split level loading reminiscent of the mine workings at Worsley.

The era of the 'Heroic Canal', from 1790 to 1820, was the boom period for canal construction and was dubbed by contemporaries as 'canal mania' (Fig 3.4). Characterised by artificial waterways which cut across the landscape via stone and iron aqueducts, along large embankments and through deep cuttings thus connecting the new industrial towns of the era (Crowe 1994, 21–2). This enthusiasm reached a peak in the years 1791–6, during which 42 new canal projects, requiring a capital outlay of £6,500,000 were put forward. Many were unrealistic projects which were quickly abandoned (Hadfield and Boughey 1998, 82–96; Table 1) but in the North West seven of these projects were built. Local landowners and industrialists continued to be the prime movers behind the promotion of many of these new canal schemes. The leading promoter of the Rochdale Canal was Mr Richard Townley of Belfield Hall in Rochdale (Holden 1979, 7–8), whilst the principle shareholders in the Manchester, Bolton and Bury Canal were the Earl of Derby, the Earl of Wilton, Sir J E Heathcote and Dr James Bert (Waterson 1988, 4–5). Samuel Oldknow, a local textile millowner who had invested his profits in land around the Marple area was the chief share holder in the Peak Forest Canal. In the era of 'canal mania' shares were bought by a large cross-section of Georgian society, from Dukes to vicars, from widows to craftsmen (Crowe 1994, 18). By the 1800s even local town councils such as

Fig 3.3 Canal Locks at Bunbury Wharf. The late eighteenth-century locks at Bunbury Wharf on the Chester and Ellesmere Canal (later part of the Shropshire Union) with their stone quoins, large wooden gates and cluster of ancillary brick buildings (stables, warehouses and company offices) are a good example of the new canal infrastructure of the late eighteenth and early nineteenth centuries.

Kendal and Liverpool were promoting the building of canals as a way of boosting local trade (Wilson 1968, 132–4).

The economic potential of the canal was outlined in a paper written in 1791 promoting the Lancaster Canal, a scheme that had first been proposed in the late 1760s. 'With Respect to Kendal, Lancaster, and perhaps Preston, it is now no longer a Question of Choice, but Necessity;-either they must put themselves on a Footing with their Southern Neighbours, or submit to a decline of their Trade and Population, and a Decrease in the Value of their Land, as a natural and inevitable Consequence: In short, a Canal is now become as

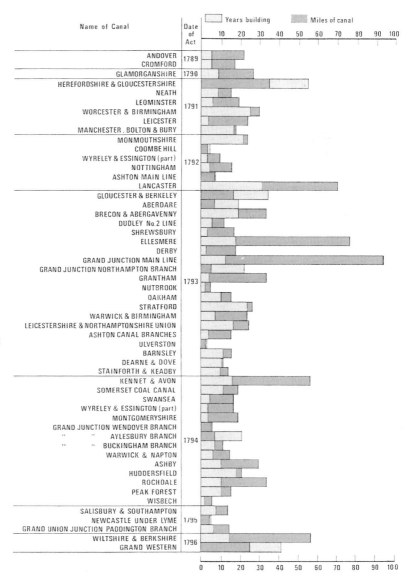

Fig 3.4 The Canal Mania (after Ransom 1979, page 42). Table showing the mileage of canals built in England and Wales as a result of Acts of Parliament passed between the years 1789 and 1796. Only those canals which were either wholly or partially built are listed, together with the years in which their last sections were opened, and the mileage of each canal as built. The Ashton, Huddersfield and Peak Forest Canals date from this period.

necessary an Appendage to a Manufacturing or Commercial Town as a Turnpike Road' (Hadfield and Biddle 1970, 184).

After 1820 the construction of canals declined, discouraged by the financial failure of some of the more speculative 'heroic' era canals as well as the rise of the railway, though the last canal to be opened, the New Junction Canal, was as late as 1905 (Crowe 1994, 22). These late canals were usually either attempts to rebuild older canals or schemes to avoid earlier congested waterways. The Manchester and Salford Junction Canal, at only ⅝ of a mile long and opened in 1839 was a classic example of this latter type. Other late canals in the North West included the Carlisle, opened in 1823, the Macclesfield, opened in 1831, and the Runcorn to Weston branch of the Bridgewater Canal opened in 1859. The Manchester Ship Canal, opened in 1894 and 36 miles long, was the exception in this period, in terms of its sheer conception and scale.

Thomas Telford, one of the great 'heroic age' canal engineers who worked extensively in the North West building amongst other things the winged warehouse at Ellesmere Port, summarised their value in 1804 in the following manner; 'It will be found that Canals are chiefly useful for the following purposes: '1st, For conveying the produce of Mines to the Sea-shore. 2nd, Conveying Fuel and Raw materials to some Manufacturing Towns and Districts, and exporting the Manufactured Goods. 3rd, Conveying Groceries and Merchant-goods for the Consumption of the District through which the Canal passes. 4th, Conveying Fuel for Domestic Purposes; Manure for the purposes of Agriculture; transporting the produce of the Districts through which the Canal passes, to the different Markets; and promoting Agricultural Purposes in general.' (Hadfield 1969, 33–4).

The real success of the canal system lay in the contrast between the amount that the average pack horse or stage wagon on the new macadamed turnpike roads could carry, roughly one eighth of a tonne and two tonnes respectively, and the amount a canal barge could ferry (Fig 3.5), which was between 30 and 100 tonnes (Crowe 1994, 16–7; Hadfield and Boughey 1998, 21–2). Thus canals allowed the raw materials of the industrial revolution, coal, clay, cotton, iron ore and limestone, to be transported cheaply and regularly to the industrial heartlands, and conversely, the finished products of these industries to be distributed via the new canal system to their markets (Fig 3.6; Armstrong 1989, 96).

Fig 3.5 Canal Boat. Modern canal boat design differs little from that in the heyday of the canal system and was determined by the width and length of the canal locks. This example, the Keppel seen here at Church Lawton Wharf on the Trent and Mersey Canal in summer 2000, is a narrow boat designed to fit into locks that are only 7 foot 6 inches wide. These were the size of locks used on the Ashton, Huddersfield and Peak Forest Canals.

Fig 3.6 Jib Crane at Red Bull Wharf, Church Lawton, Cheshire. Cranes and hoists were a vital element of the canal infrastructure, allowing the rapid loading and unloading of canal boats. There were a number of different types of crane used on the region's canals. This example, at Red Bull Wharf, is an example of the most common type, a stand-alone jib crane which would have been worked by hand.

The Canal System in Tameside

During the boom in canal building during the 1790s three narrow-boat canals (that is canals with locks built to accommodate boats of 7ft beam) were proposed and constructed across Tameside (Fig 3.7). Since all three shared many of the same promoters, shareholders, committeemen and engineers, and even used the same Altrincham based solicitors, the Worthingtons (who also acted as agents for the Earl of Stamford), these three canals can be seen as creating one system which provided a through route for canal trade from Liverpool to Hull. Although the 'establishing and carrying on a thoroughfare Trade

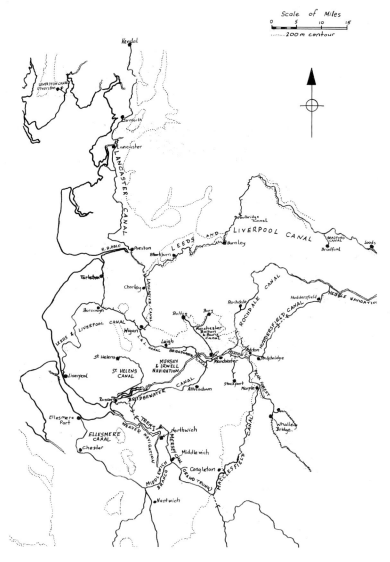

Fig 3.7 A map of the canal network in North West England, after Hadfield and Biddle 1970.

from Hull to Manchester' was the spur for co-operation between the three canals, the immediate aims of the projects were to capture local and regional trade and so boost the income of the local landowners and industrialists (Hadfield and Biddle 1970, 296–8; Schofield 1992, 5–7). As part of this aim Ashton formed a key focus for the three schemes being an important coal mining centre in this part of the Lancashire coalfield. This is indicated by the Act for the Manchester, Ashton and Oldham canal which gave coalmine owners powers to build canal branches up to four miles long, and indeed the Fairbottom branch to the Park Bridge Ironworks and Fairbottom Colliery, a length of 1¼ miles, was built using these powers (Hadfield and Biddle 1970, 298; Keaveney and Brown 1974).

Fig 3.8 Map of Ashton-under-Lyne surveyed in 1824 for Baines' Lancashire. The line of the Ashton Canal runs along the northern bank of the River Tame between the river and the town. At this date there was only one wharf in Ashton, the old wharf, which was situated south of the church (1) and Ashton Old Hall (9). The Portland Basin Warehouse at Ashton New Wharf was not built until 1834.

The Ashton Canal

The Manchester, Ashton-under-Lyne and Oldham Canal was the first to be built, construction taking place in the years 1792–7 (Fig 3.8). The backers of this canal included the Earl of Stamford, other local landowners and a group of colliery owners from the Ashton, Denton and Oldham areas. The intended course was to run from a junction with the proposed Rochdale Canal at Ducie Street in the centre of Manchester for seven miles, with 18 locks, to Ashton, where it would

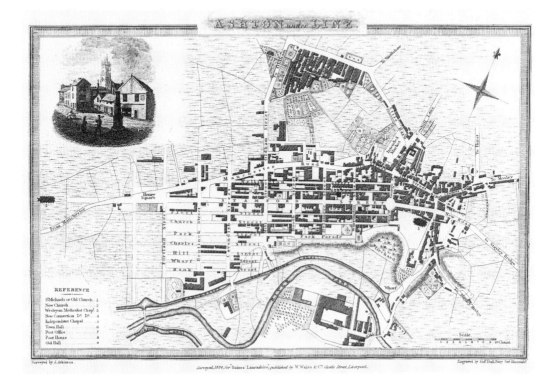

join the proposed Peak Forest Canal at the Portland Basin. There was also to be a branch heading northwards to New Mill near Oldham (Hadfield and Biddle 1970, 294; Paget-Tomlinson 1993, 98–9; Scofield 1992, 6–9).

The Act was passed on 11 June 1792 and authorised the raising of £60,000 initially, with provision for a further £30,000 on mortgage. Shares in the canal were issued soon afterwards, at a cost of £100 each, all were sold. On the 31 July 1792 the backers advertised for an engineer and Benjamin Outram was eventually appointed. In 1793 a second Act was passed authorising a branch arm from Clayton to Heaton Norris (the Stockport Arm). A further three Acts were passed between 1798 and 1805 ostensibly to raise money for minor works such as warehouses and wharves, but in reality to allow the completion of the original scheme (Schofield 1992, 8). The main warehouse was at Ducie Street in Manchester, but there was also a large warehouse built at Ashton Old Wharf and the Heaton Norris terminus of the Stockport branch.

Opening in late 1796 the Manchester to Ashton section cost approximately £170,000 (Hadfield and Biddle 1970, 464–5). The Stockport, Hollinwood and Fairbottom branches opened the following year, raising the final cost to £216,000 (more than double the original estimate) despite the fact that the Beat Bank section, which was due to link the Denton collieries to the Stockport branch, was abandoned in 1798. This was due to three factors; the escalating cost of the whole project and the financial burdens already incurred by the Ashton Canal; the opening of the Hollinwood and Fairbottom branches which gave the company access to the Werneth coal mines in Oldham and the Fairbottom coal mines in Ashton; and the rivalry for coal mine income between the Earl of Stamford in Ashton and the Fletcher family who owned coal mines in Denton (Cronin and Yearsley 1985, 68; Hadfield and Biddle 1970, 295–6; Schofield 1992, 9–10).

Direct links with other canals were planned from the very beginning; the Peak Forest Canal would give access to the limestone quarries in Derbyshire and via the Trent and Mersey the industries of the north Midlands, whilst the Huddersfield Narrow Canal would provide links with Yorkshire and the woollen districts. However, these links were slow in appearing. The long delayed completion of the Rochdale Canal from the Dale Street Basin to the Bridgewater Canal in 1804/5 gave access to Yorkshire, and it was not until 1804 that the opening of the Peak Forest Canal through the Marple lock flight gave the Ashton Canal links with the north Midlands via the Trent and Mersey Canal. The Huddersfield Narrow Canal was not completed until 1811 (Scofield 1992, 10–1).

Despite the financial difficulties of its first decade of existence tonnage and profits on the canal expanded continually throughout the first third of the nineteenth century reaching a peak in 1838 (Owen 1977; Table 2). In that year 514,241 tons were carried, from coal and cotton to vegetables, grain and people, bringing in an income of £17,363, and a dividend of 7% was paid to shareholders. This steady expansion necessitated the building of a new warehouse at Ashton New Wharf, now the Portland Basin.

Table 2: Ashton Canal Tonnage and Revenue

Year	Tonnage	Revenue
1828	274,629	£10,736
1838	514,241	£17,363
1848	469,108	£11,443
1858	433,526	£9,570
1905	241,176	£8,203
1934	21,195	£621

Source: Owen 1977, 78–80.

The Peak Forest Canal

The backers of the Ashton Canal had considered financing the construction of the Peak Forest Canal through the Ashton Canal Company. It was decided that this would be too great a financial commitment and a separate company was formed, the final cost being £177,000 (Hadfield and Biddle 1970, 306; 312). The route of the Peak Forest Canal ran from near Portland Basin to Woodley and Marple through to a terminus at Bugsworth (now Buxworth), with a short branch to Whaley Bridge (Fig 3.9). A tramroad connected the Bugsworth terminus with the limestone quarries at Dove Holes because of the very hilly terrain. It rose 209 feet via sixteen locks, from Portland Basin to Marple. Not only was the canal designed to carry limestone, but it's line also exploited the coal traffic in Dukinfield and Hyde (Hadfield and Biddle 1970, 306–7). Benjamin Outram was appointed the engineer. For this venture the largest and most important shareholder was Samuel Oldknow, a local landowner and mill owner (Paget-Tomlinson 1993, 178–9).

Construction began in 1794 and in the autumn of 1797 the upper level of the canal, from Bugsworth to Marple Basin, was opened. A year later the lower level of the canal, from the Marple Aqueduct to Dukinfield and the Portland Basin, was also opened. To reduce the costs it was decided to use a tramway to link the lower and upper pounds at Marple instead of using locks. Because the demand for

Fig 3.9 Roving bridge over the Peak Forest Canal, Hyde.
Roving bridges are a common element of canal architecture and serve the purpose of combining a bridge and a change of bank for the tow path. They are distinguished by a curved incline, which rises to the bridge, with a straight incline on the other side. This design allowed towing horses to cross over without being unhitched.

limestone was so great the tramway was unable to cope with the traffic so as a result a further 16 locks were built along this stretch; these were opened in 1804. The main traffic along the canal was coal, lime and limestone; 291 narrow boats were loaded with limestone during one period of four weeks in 1824.

The Huddersfield Narrow Canal

The last canal to be opened in Tameside was the Huddersfield Narrow Canal (Paget-Tomlinson 1993, 146–7). It was constructed in the years 1794–1811 with the intention of capturing cross-Pennine trade from Hull to Manchester, in particular the traffic of coal, corn, lime, and limestone (Hadfield and Biddle 1970, 331). Benjamin Outram was at first appointed as engineer but later Thomas Telford undertook surveys and proposed improvements to the canal's course (Fig 3.10). The route chosen ran from the eastern end of the Ashton Canal at Ashton Old Wharf up the Tame valley and across the Pennines to Sir John Ramsden's broad canal at Cooper Bridge near Huddersfield. The nearly 20 mile length of the canal rose 338 feet through 32 locks above its Ashton start, culminating

in the Standedge tunnel, originally three miles and 198 yards long. It then descended 493 feet from Marsden, through 42 locks, to Huddersfield (Hadfield and Biddle 1970, 322–3).

The Ashton to Stalybridge section opened in November 1796, and that stretch from Stalybridge to Uppermill in August 1797. In 1793 the cost had been estimated at £178,748, with five years needed to cut the Standedge Tunnel, which alone finally cost over £160,000. As the tunnel took 17 years to build the full length of the canal did not open until March 1811; and the final cost of the project was over £400,000. Furthermore, the rival Rochdale Canal, which gave a Pennine route fifteen miles shorter, had been built and opened over six years previously (Hadfield and Biddle 1970, 328–9). The long term result was a price war with the Rochdale and continuing financial problems for the Huddersfield Canal Company.

The Tameside Canals in the Later Nineteenth Century

By the 1830's all three Tameside canals were enjoying a period of sustained prosperity with rising traffic tonnage as well as annual dividends being paid to shareholders. The success of the Liverpool and Manchester Railway, opened in 1830 and making substantial profits by 1831, marked the beginning of the end of the canal building age; although serious competition was not to take place in the North West until the railway boom of the 1840s. From the 1820s the canal companies were increasingly aware of the potential threat from the railways, at first seeing them as a useful adjunct to their business, but increasingly as rivals. Thus, in 1826 the Peak Forest Canal Company welcomed the proposed Cromford and High Peak Railway 'which if made and completed would be of great benefit to this Canal' (Hadfield and Biddle 1970, 314). In contrast in 1825 the Huddersfield Canal Company had threatened the Ashton Canal Company with the promotion of 'a new communication by Rail Road or otherwise from the Huddersfield Canal to Manchester' if the Ashton did not convert their canal to double locks so as to ease traffic congestion (Hadfield and Biddle 1970, 302).

The trans-Pennine rail proposals of the 1840s, from Manchester to Leeds via Standedge, and from Manchester to Sheffield via Woodhead, marked the end of commercial independence for the Tameside canals and the beginning of a protracted period of decline. Canals could not compete with the speed of railway transport, nor with the flexibility of the network, handicapped as they were by the lack of through tolls due to the absence of a central clearing booking scheme such as the railways used (Paget-Tomlinson 1993, 5). As profits and tonnage

Fig 3.10 Stakes Aqueduct, Stalybridge. This view of the Stakes Aqueduct, on the Huddersfield Canal, shows the cast-iron trough which forms the canal (centre), with the arched stone tow path bridge just visible on the left. The construction of this aqueduct over the River Tame in 1800 was one of the earliest instances of the use of such a cast-iron trough in the country.

dwindled canals were bought by railway companies, either to get rid of competition and opposition or to build their own lines on (Paget-Tomlinson 1993, 5). Tameside's first canal to be bought by a railway company was the least successful; the Huddersfield Canal Company was sold to the Huddersfield and Manchester Railway in 1844, who then changed their name to the Huddersfield and Manchester Railway and Canal Company. The canal was later leased to the LNWR in 1847 (Hadfield and Biddle 1970, 335). Shortly afterwards in 1846 and 1848 both the Peak Forest Canal Company and the Ashton Canal Company were sold to the Sheffield, Ashton-under-Lyne and Manchester Railway, who's Manchester terminus lay adjacent to the Ducie Street canal basin (Hadfield and Biddle 1970, 305, 315).

All three canals continued in service. Traffic tonnage on the Ashton canal, though halved compared to 1838, was still around 240,000 tons per year in 1905, the most important goods carried being coal at over 102,000 tons that year (Hadfield and Biddle 1970, 442). Railway companies were not interested in the long term future of the canals. In 1893 the Great Central Railway, successor to the Manchester, Sheffield and Lincolnshire Railway, ceased to operate its canal fleet and cut its maintenance of the Ashton Canal, particularly dredging. At the same time the costs of transport on the canals were raised. However, it was the rapid growth of road haulage in the 1920s, coupled with colliery subsidence along the route in Hollinwood and Fairbottom, that destroyed commercial traffic on the Ashton Canal, and in 1958 all commercial traffic ceased. Neglect and vandalism meant that by 1960 the canal was unnavigable (Owen 1977).

The Peak Forest Canal was at first the most successful of the canals under railway ownership, the limestone business of the Doveholes quarries remaining profitable until the end of the nineteenth century. In 1883 the Manchester, Sheffield and Lincolnshire Railway took over the canal. As the quarries declined so did the fortunes of the canal, the railway company giving up its own fleet of canal boats in 1893. By 1905 tonnage per year was down from *c.* 378,000 in 1858 to 136,000, the last loads of limestone being carried in 1925, when the tramway was closed. Although this was partially offset by the promotion of pleasure traffic, by 1948 the canal had fallen into dereliction (Hadfield and Biddle 1970, 444–5; Owen 1977, 75–6; Paget-Tomlinson 1993, 178–9).

Traffic along the Huddersfield Canal had remained between 200,000 and 150,000 tons per year until the end of the nineteenth century. Although regular through traffic ceased around 1905 the lowland western and eastern ends of this canal continued to be actively used until the First World War, and were only abandoned by the London and North Western Railway in 1944 (Hadfield and Biddle 1970, 445–7).

Twentieth-century Decline

The ever-widening development of the railway network, the poor wages paid to boatmen, the decline in maintenance standards and the development of road transport all took their toll on the canal network during the first half of the twentieth century. Men leaving to fight during the First World War accelerated the decline in canal traffic. In 1913, 31,588,909 tons were carried on British Canals. This had declined to 21,599,850 tons in 1918, and fell steadily during the mid-twentieth century, to 17m tons in 1924 and 13m tons in 1938 (Hadfield and Boughey 1998, 243). The dislocation of trade routes in the early years of the Second World War caused a fall in trade to 11m tons, half of which was coal.

The Second World War had left Britain's canals under-used and badly maintained. Consequently in January 1948 the British Transport Commission took over most of the independently owned waterways (Hadfield and Boughey 1998, 260). Throughout the 1950s there was still substantial use, particularly in the Birmingham area where there was over 1m tons of short-haul traffic every year, but by the early 1960s most of this had gone, because of the opening of motorways and the closure of collieries. In 1962 an independent body, the British Waterways Board, was set up to manage the nationalized inland waterways and the growing transition from transportation to amenity uses (Hadfield and Boughey 1998, 262–4).

The Surviving Canal Fabric

All three of the canal routes in Tameside still survive as navigable water-courses, having been restored for pleasure traffic in the 1960s and 1970s (Owen 1977, 80). This includes 18 locks on the main stretch of the Ashton Canal. Although the Hollinwood, Fairbottom and Stockport branches are no longer navigable much can still be seen. The whole of the Peak Forest Canal can still be traversed and most of the Huddersfield Canal, except for a short stretch through Stalybridge town centre, although this too is now being restored and is due to be opened to pleasure traffic in 2002.

Much of the related late eighteenth- and early nineteenth-century infrastructure of the canals, from locks and tow paths to warehouses and wharfs can still be seen, though their survival is fragmentary

Fig 3.11 Bridge over the Peak Forest Canal, Portland Basin, Ashton. According to the datestone on the bridge it was erected in 1835. This arched tow path bridge straddles the junction between the Ashton and Peak Forest Canals. The shallow gradient of the bridge produces a structure of some elegance.

(Burke and Nevell 1996). The best place to see most of these secondary elements still *in situ* is at the Portland Basin, the heart of the canal system in Tameside. Here at the junction of the Ashton and Peak Forest canals, which were opened in 1796 and 1797, is a fine single arched towpath bridge of 1835 spanning the Peak Forest Canal (Fig 3.11), which is carried over the river Tame by a three-arch sandstone aqueduct, designed and built by Benjamin Outram and Thomas Brown (Fig 3.12). To the north is the restored Portland Basin Warehouse of 1835 and to the east of the junction, across the Ashton Canal,

Fig 3.12 The Peak Forest Canal aqueduct. This fine three-arched sandstone aqueduct, was designed and built by Benjamin Outram and Thomas Brown, and was opened in 1797. It carried the peak Forect Canal over the River Tame to its junction with the Ashton Canal (on the left below the 1835 arched-bridge).

Fig 3.13 Lock keeper's cottage, Fairfield Top Lock, Droylsden. This house by the Ashton Canal is possibly as early as the 1790s and was originally built as a canal agent's house. The composed, symmetrical brick-built facade is very much in keeping with reserved contemporary Georgian taste.

there is a steel footbridge, dating from the 1950's, which replaced an original timber footbridge built by Isaac Watt Boulton in 1843.

The range of buildings associated with canals includes lock keepers' cottages, toll houses and warehouses. In Tameside the architecture of the lock keepers' cottages is plain and functional, with little evidence of architectural embellishment. The buildings by Fairfield Top Lock, on the Ashton Canal in Droylsden, form one of the most impressive collections of canal structures within Tameside. Included within this group are two lock keepers' cottages built in the 1790s, one of which was originally a canal agent's house (Figs 3.13 and Fig 3.14). Both are two-storey, brick buildings with centrally placed doorways. The symmetrical facade of the canal agent's house is in keeping with its reserved Georgian style. The nearby toll house has coped gables and

Fig 3.14 Canal toll house, Fairfield Top Lock, Droylsden. This early nineteenth-century building on the Ashton Canal contains only office facilities, with no provision for domestic accommodation. It has a plain, functional, design.

a ball finial, but is otherwise plain. The boathouse, which has a datestone of 1833, is a long, low, building in stone with a coped gable and kneelers and a keystone arch (Fig 3.15).

The most impressive buildings associated with the canals in Tameside are the warehouses, and of these the examples at Portland Basin and Hyde Wharf are the best survivals. The Hyde Wharf Warehouse, built in 1828 and now converted for office use (Fig 3.16), is particularly attractive, with loading bays on three sides and a symmetrical arrangement of brick arched windows. Stone dressing and coped gables

dignify this three-storey brick building. The 1834 warehouse at Portland Basin, despite suffering large-scale damage as a result of fire, has been recently rebuilt and once more provides an impressive backdrop to the junction of the Ashton and Peak Forest canals.

The bridges associated with canals fall into two categories; those which carry roads or tow paths over a canal; and the aqueducts which carry the canal over a particular obstacle. The most attractive road bridges across canals are the roving bridges, which allow towing horses to cross the canal without being unhitched and are characterized by a spiral tow path on one side. A good example of a roving bridge is the Manchester Road Canal Bridge in Hyde, on the Peak Forest Canal. It is constructed in stone with stone setts on the path. The 1835 tow path bridge over the Peak Forest Canal at its junction with the Ashton Canal is notable for its graceful design, with a low, elongated span; and with the Ashton Canal Warehouse forms an attractive architectural assemblage at this confluence of two major waterways.

Canal aqueducts, particularly those spanning rivers, were regarded as structures of curiosity and were often both picturesque and monumental in design. The aqueducts within Tameside are relatively conservative in design, in part due to the absence of major obstacles to the canals within the Borough. The most significant structure is the Stakes Aqueduct over the River Tame in Stalybridge. It was built in 1800 and consists of a cast-iron trough which carries the Huddersfield Canal over the river. This replaced an earlier stone-built aqueduct and is one of the earliest examples of its type in the country. By contrast, the aqueduct which carries the Peak Forest Canal over the River Tame is a sturdy triple arched structure built in stone and brick.

Building on the Past

The collapse of Britain's canal network in the middle of the twentieth century meant than many fine and unique buildings were lost. In the North West some of the most historically important canal structures of the industrial age were swept away by fire (Telford's unique winged warehouse of 1835) or for redevelopment (the first warehouse, the Duke's in Castlefield, the iron-framed Grain Warehouse in Liverpool and the unusual Bury Wharf warehouse were all demolished as redundant buildings). Stretches of canal were filled in and built over; the site of the Bolton Canal terminus and the line of the canal south of there for two miles are now occupied by the dual carriageway known as St Peter's Way and the line of the Stockport branch of the Ashton Canal has been largely built over by housing. In Tameside most of the original canal network survives and fine buildings including the 1833 boathouse on the Ashton Canal at Droylsden or the 1828 warehouse on the Peak Forest Canal in Hyde have been saved, restored and protected as Listed Buildings. The Ashton and Peak Forest Canals now form part of the 'Cheshire Ring' and from 2002 the stretch of the Huddersfield Narrow Canal filled in through the centre of Stalybridge will be re-open, uniting the Yorkshire and Lancashire halves of the canal for the first time in nearly 100 years.

4

Pheonix from the Ashes

The Fall and Rise of Portland Basin

The textile and mining industries of the area had always provided the main trade for the canals of Tameside, and as these declined in the first half of the twentieth century so did the commercial life of the Ashton, Huddersfield and Peak Forest Canals and, consequently, so did that of the Portland Basin Warehouse. In 1905 the Ashton Canal carried 241,176 tons, nearly half of which was coal. This had declined to 23,077 tons by 1931 and in 1947 the main line from Manchester to Ashton carried just 5,452 tons (Hadfield and Biddle 1970, 442; Keveaney and Brown 1974, 30). After the Second World War the collapse in commercial traffic was followed by the rapid closure of the canal network across Tameside. The Huddersfield Canal was closed in 1944 (Hadfield and Biddle 1970, 447) and the main branch of the Ashton Canal became unnavigable around 1960. Whilst the upper 3.5 miles of the Hollinwood branch was closed in 1955 the rest stayed open until 1961. The Stockport branch had ceased carrying commercial traffic in the 1930s and was formerly closed in 1962. By the 1960s all commercial activity had ceased on the canals, which along with the Portland Basin Warehouse, lay derelict.

The canals of the Tameside area could have been filled in and forgotten (the British Transport Commission had drafted a bill to close the Ashton and Peak Forest Canals although this was never passed by Parliament). During the mid to late 1960s and early 1970s the rise in popularity of the new subject of Industrial Archaeology sparked interest in the 200 year old canal network of Britain. In 1964 the Peak Forest Canal Society was formed and along with the Inland Waterways Association began to fight to keep the Peak Forest and Ashton Canals open, with the ultimate intention of restoring them and the 'Cheshire Ring', the group of canals that circled the old county of Cheshire of which the Ashton and Peak Forest formed the north-eastern sections (Keaveney and Brown 1974, 32). In September 1968, in one of the first large-scale actions of its kind in the country, and certainly the most celebrated, 600 volunteers arrived from all over England and Wales to take part in the large scale clearance along a 700 yard length of the Ashton Canal ending at Fairfield Locks. In one weekend 2,000 tonnes of rubbish were removed from the canal demonstrating the effectiveness of such volunteer actions (Hadfield and Boughey 1998, 273–4).

Continued campaigning led to the adoption in 1971 of a scheme to fully restore the Ashton Canal between Manchester and Ashton. With the active support of the British Waterways Board, and money from Audenshaw Council, Ashton Council, the Inland Waterways Association, Lancashire County Council, Manchester City Council and the Peak Forest Canal the clearance and restoration of the full canal began with over 1,000 volunteers in one weekend in early 1972. It took two years for the British Waterways Board team, lead by John Freeman the area engineer for Wigan, to clear the Ashton Canal, with much assistance by volunteers from a variety of societies. The canal was re-opened for navigation on 1 April 1974 having cost £300,000 to restore, which included the removal of over 100,000 tonnes of rubbish dredged from the canal, and the repair of all the locks and three aqueducts (Keaveney and Brown 1974, 33–4).

The restoration of the Peak Forest Canal had begun in earnest in 1964 with the formation of the Peak Forest Canal Society who's initial aim was to save the Marple aqueduct, which had partially collapsed in 1962. In 1965 the first volunteer clearing parties set to work and in 1971 permission was given to restore the lower section of the canal,

Fig 4.1 Portland Basin in 1985.
A view of the southern, canal side, facade of the Portland Basin warehouse in 1985. The warehouse was burnt down in 1972 but in 1985 a small museum was opened by Tameside MBC in the eastern half of the ruins.

Fig 4.2 Portland Basin in 1999.
In March 1999 the Portland Basin was re-opened as a social and industrial history museum, with the upper storeys of the warehouse being rebuilt to its original design.

from Portland Basin to the Marple locks, at the same time as the restoration of the Ashton Canal. This section was finally re-opened in 1974 (Hadfield and Boughey 198, 303). Since then Tameside's canal network has been further restored with the re-opening of the full length of the Peak Forest Canal culminating in 1999 with the completion of the restoration works at the Bugsworth Basin. In 2001 the Huddersfield Narrow Canal will be opened through Stalybridge, restoring this historic trans-Pennine link.

It was ironic that whilst the Ashton and Peak Forest canals were being restored the Portland Basin warehouse was facing destruction. In 1972 the warehouse was devastated by a fire which started in a store holding paints and solvents. This destroyed much of the building and left the warehouse in ruins, the top two storeys being demolished as unsafe. The future of the rest of the building remained in doubt throughout the 1970s and was only finally secured when it was acquired by Tameside MBC in the early 1980s (Fig 4.1).

The council then embarked on a two phase restoration programme. The initial phase, opened in 1985, saw the building of a small Heritage Centre and Museum in the eastern ground floor half of the building, whilst the rest of the site lay in a ruinous condition (Fig 4.2; Delve 1997, 50). This initial restoration project also included the rebuilding of the external waterwheel which was undertaken by

Dorothea Restorations Ltd of Whaley Bridge in 1988 which involved the replacement of the main wheel spokes and some of the iron buckets. Much of the original 1840s cast iron wheel was salvageable, including the central bearing and most of the buckets (Fig 4.3). The fully restored wheel was winched into place in April 1988. The second phase of the restoration project, which began in 1997, involved rebuilding the warehouse to its original height and design at a cost of £8m (Delve 1997, 51). The fully restored warehouse was opened in March 1999 and the much enlarged museum occupies the whole of the first and second storeys, whilst the third storey and roof space are occupied by a conference suite and domestic flats. A wider scheme of restoration around Ashton New Wharf, encompassing the tow paths, bridges and the provision of sign boards, was undertaken at the same time as the warehouse restoration, along with the conversion of the nearby canal side Cavendish Mill. The expanded museum thus sits within a wider historic canal landscape that is not only a popular navigation but through Ashton-under-Lyne is a linear industrial park.

Fig 4.3 A fragment of the original 1840s waterwheel. The rebuilding of the external waterwheel which was undertaken by Dorothea Restorations Ltd of Whaley Bridge in 1988 and involved the replacement of the main wheel spokes and some of the iron buckets. Much of the original 1840s cast iron wheel was salvageable, including the central bearing and most of the buckets, although this fragment was not included in the final restoration project. The fully restored wheel was winched into place in April 1988.

Fig 4.4 The new museum.
The enlarged museum describes the social, political and industrial history of the Tameside area. Visitors enter on the upper level of the museum where the Social History Gallery is housed, whilst the Industrial Gallery is located on the lower floor, from where there is access to the canal side.

The Museum

The enlarged museum describes the social, political and industrial history of the Tameside area. Visitors enter on the upper level of the museum (Fig 4.4) where the Social History Gallery is housed. This explores the social and economic history of Tameside from family, housing and migration to health, retailing, religion and recreation. Central to this part of the museum is the recreation of a Tameside street scene from the 1920s featuring the furnished downstairs rooms of a typical terraced house, a school room, fish and chip shop, grocer's shop, a workshop, public house, chapel and classroom.

The Industrial Gallery is located on the lower floor and covers the history of Tameside over the last four centuries. 'Made in Tameside' is the central exhibition and includes displays about the goods manufactured or produced in the Tameside area from coalmining, glove making and hatting to textiles and engineering. There is a separate exhibition on the excavations of the seventeenth-century glass furnaces at Glass House Fold in Haughton and there is a special section on the development of canal transport in the region, which includes some of the fixtures and fittings salvaged from the Portland Basin Warehouse before the fire, including a jib crane, hoist and clerk's desk.

Building for the Future

The dominance of motor transport in the twentieth century led to a shift away from canal and railway transport, and consequently by 1960 most of Britain's canals, and their associated locks, bridges, boat houses and warehouses lay derelict. Though much of the 200 year old network was destroyed in the following decade many of these canal buildings, and the canals themselves, were saved in the 1970s and 1980s by vigorous local campaigns and by British Waterways working with local government and volunteer support in their restoration. The historical importance of the artificial waterways of the Industrial Revolution was recognised nationally when in 1988 British

Waterways and English Heritage began an architectural heritage survey of England's canals directed by Dr Nigel Crowe and in 1993 he became British Waterways' first Heritage Manager. At the start of the twenty-first century much of the canal network of Britain survives, and is in daily use for the leisure industry. The restoration of buildings such as Portland Basin ensures that these linear industrial monuments will retain their unique waterside character for many years to come.

A Gazetteer of the Surviving Canal Warehouses of North West England

The following sites were visited specifically for this volume and represent those buildings known at the time of the survey to be have been built as canal warehouses.

Cheshire

Bunbury Locks

SJ 578 590

7.4m × 12.1m, 179m², Type 2

Built *c.*1880 by canal company. Two storey, 3 bays × 1 bay, machine-brick warehouse in EGW (English Garden Wall) bond. Large central loading bay doors to first and second floors on the northern canal side, with stone steps to first floor. Bull-nosed corners at south-western and south-eastern corners. Single loading bay door on the roadside, southern elevation. Internally the floors are wooden supported by two transverse beams. On southern side of the Shropshire Union Canal by the locks.

Bunbury Locks

Chester Steam Mills

SJ 413 666

9.2m × 25.5 (+ 9.2m × 17.2m), 1408m², later 2199m², Type 2

Built *c.*1850 and *c.*1880. Range of three, five and six-storey brick buildings on the southern side of the canal forming part a large urban corn-mill complex. Along the western side of the eastern main building is a six storey, brick canal warehouse with 3 bays fronting the canal (the central one containing loading bay doors, and the remains of a hoist at the top) and 8 bays running south from the canal, with further loading bays. The windows are rectangular with shallow brick arched lintels and stone sills. Wooden floor supported by cast-iron columns. Attached to the rear are two five brick storey additions of 2 and 3 bays each. On the Shropshire Union Canal.

Chester, Telford's Warehouse, Tower Wharf

SJ 401 667

17m × 14.4m, c.734m², Type 1

Built *c.*1830 by canal company. Brick-built, warehouse in EGW bond of 3 bays × 9 bays with a hipped, slate roof. Road side is three

Chester, Telford's Warehouse

storeys but the canal side (which has stone quoins) is four storeys, the bottom storey being occupied by a boat loading arm which runs past the southern and eastern elevations. Loading bay doors in the western elevation. Originally a rectangular structure, a short western two storey brick wing was later added. This runs out over the canal so that the lower level forms an extension of the canal loading arm, which stands on brick arches on stone piers. On the Shropshire Union Canal.

Church Lawton, Red Bull Wharf

SJ 828 551

28.9m × 6.12m, 530.6m², Type 2

Built *c.* 1850 by the canal company. Three-storey, 5 bays × 1 bay, brick-built warehouse

in EGW bond. Square windows with segmented brick arches and stone sills. King post supporting a pitched roof. Single span with wooden floors supported by transverse beams. Separate crane on the canal tow path. Recently restored as offices for the Waterways Board. On the Hall Green branch (opened 1831) of the Trent and Mersey Canal.

Congleton Wharf

SJ 866 622

21.8m × 8m, 523.2m², Type 3

Built *c.* 1831 by canal company. Three-storey, brick-built warehouse, of 7 bays × 1 bay in EGW bond. Square windows with segmental brick arches and stone sills. Pitched slate roof, and central loading openings on the canal front (bay 4). Central loading bay on the road side with a pediment above. Single span with wooden floors supported by posts. On the Macclesfield Canal.

Ellesmere Port, Island Grain Warehouse

SJ 406 773, LBII

30.5m × 51.6m, c. 3148m², Type 1

Built 1871 by the canal company. Island Grain Warehouse is a large rectangular, two storey, brick building with three aisles, 15 bays long, six loading openings on the north-eastern front, main area of the Boat Museum.

Church Lawton, Red Bull Wharf.

The Island Grain Warehouse at Ellesmere Port.

Brown brick with blue brick projecting piers and bands on the north-west, north-east and south-eastern sides. Grey slate roof with three parallel ridges terminating in gables at the south-east and north-west of the building. The first floor of the south-western bay is carried over a covered loading bay, through which one arm of the canal passes with cast-iron columns supporting walls over the loading bay. Internal floors are supported by cast-iron columns and wooden beams. At the Mersey end of the Ellesmere and Chester (later Shropshire Union) Canal. Now the home of The Boat Museum (CSMR 6).

Ellesmere Port, China Clay Shed

SJ 405 773, LBII

54m × 14.1m, c. 761.4m², Type 2

Built 1846 by the canal company. China Clay and Bone Ash Warehouse is built on an island formed by the canal, the basin and an arm of the canal. It has a single storey, double-depth plan with red and blue brick walls and a slate roof. Circular openings filled with cast iron wheel grilles, with radiating spokes on gable pediments. The warehouse was used for the storage of china clay, shipped by coasted from Cornwall, then transported by narrow boat to the Potteries. Bone ash, for bone china, was similarly stored

and transported. At the Mersey end of the Ellesmere and Chester (later Shropshire Union) Canal.

Lymm, Heatley Wharf

SJ 705 873

21m × 7m, 441m², Type 3

Built *c.* 1800 by the canal company. Three-storey, brick-built warehouse in EGW bond, of 1 bay × 4 bays, aligned lengthways to the southern side of the Bridgewater Canal. Square windows with segmented arched windows and stone sills. King post roof, single span with wooden floors supported by large transverse beams. Loading bay in bay 3 on southern, roadside, elevation, with the remains of a cathead and crane below the slate pitched roof. Loading bay on canal side flanked by ocular openings. On the Trent and Mersey Canal.

Middlewich Wharf

SJ 705 662

6.9m × 18.35m, 379.9m², Type 2

Built *c.* 1870 by the canal company. Three-storey, brick-built, warehouse, whitewashed, pitched roof, three-storey loading opening on east end wall. On the Trent and Mersey Canal.

Heatley Wharf.

Middlewich Wharf.

Preston Brook Wharf.

Preston Brook Wharf

SJ 568 805

10.55m × 38.1m, 1206m², Type 2

Built *c.* 1830 by the canal company. Three storey brick warehouse 15 bays by 2 bays, aligned lengthwise to the canal, hipped slate roof. Roadside, which has two taking-in doors, has two storeys, but canal side, which has three loading bays with remains of cat-heads, has three storeys. Loading bay in eastern gable. Rectangular windows with stone sills and ornamental stone lintels, iron frames with small panes. Internally cast-iron columns carry the timber floor and the roof has massive beams. Projecting wooden load-ing bay supported on cast iron pillars on canal front has been rebuilt in timber (CSMR 98/1). Now converted to flats. On the Trent and Mersey Canal.

Cumbria

Kendal, Canal Head Warehouses

SD 510 920

17.14m × 37.4m, 1282m², Type 1

Built 1819 by the local town council and the canal company. Stone built, two storey block of two contemporary warehouses, each 55 by 60 feet, 1 bay × 4 bays, in plan, with arched internal loading bays entered from the east.

Sandbach, Wheelock Wharf I

SJ 751 593

20.45m × 6.35m, c. 389.6m², Type 2

Built *c.* 1800. Three-storey, brick-built, ware-house west of the road bridge of 1 bay × 6 bays. King post roof. Cast-iron columns are later additions. Semi-circular arched windows, loading doors on road front. Five tie-bars, two loading openings on the canal side. Cathead cranes on the road side. Central pediment. Converted to a corn-mill in the late nineteenth century. Now occupied by garden centre. On the Trent and Mersey Canal.

Sandbach, Wheelock Wharf II

SJ 752 593

8.1m × 7.2m and 7.8m × 9.5m, 397.3m², Type 2

Built *c.* 1800 by the canal company. Two and a half storeys, brick-built, two phased ware-house east of the road bridge. Square windows with segmented brick arches and stone sills. King post roof. Two loading bays on the canal side and a single cart entrance in the western gable. Single span with wooden floors supported by transverse beams. 1 bay × 5 bays, the western 2 bays appear to be the earlier building. Canal offices at the western end of the range by the bridge. Recently converted to a restaurant. On the Trent and Mersey Canal.

On the western, landward side are large door-ways opening onto loading-bays facing Bridge Street. The northern wing was a stable block for the barge horses, and the southern wing were cottages, perhaps for warehouse labourers. Around 1900 they were incorpor-ated within the Canal Iron Works complex and substantially altered. On the Lancaster Canal.

Greater Manchester

Altrincham, Broadheath

SJ 765 890

20m × 23m, 1380m², Type 1

Built 1833 by canal company. Three storey brick-built warehouse of 5 bays × 5 bays, with a hipped roof, on the southern side of the Bridgewater Canal. Single, central, canal loading arm in northern elevation, surmounted by a classical pediment. Cart loading entrance in middle of southern elevation, also surmounted by a classical pediment. Two loading bays in eastern gable, with cathead surviving. Later warehouse building of 3 bays × 5 bays added to the west.

Ashton-under-Lyne, Portland Basin (New Wharf)

SJ 934 985

22m × 61m, c.4026m², Type 1

Built 1834 by canal company. Three storey, brick-built, warehouse of 1834 (datestone), with two central loading bays. Wooden floors supported by cast-iron columns. Waterwheel for hoists added in 1841. Most of the warehouse was destroyed by fire in 1972. The ground floor with its loading bays, part of the water-wheel power system and cast-iron columns, are original. The rest is a reconstruction of 1998–99. At the junction of the Ashton Canal and Peak Forest Canal.

Bury Coal Wharf

SD 797 110

15.8m × 14.5m, 916m², Type 1

Built 1824–9 by local industrialist. The Bury terminus of the Manchester Bolton and Bury Canal was opened in 1797 on the southern side of Bury Bridge. Although the original wharf with its two, three storey, warehouses has gone a privately built warehouse survives on the eastern side of the private 1824 extension north of Bury Bridge. Four storey, 4 bays × 3 bays, stone-built structure, with

Altrincham, Broadheath.

Waterwheel at Portland Basin.

two arched, keystone boat holes. Keystone arch cart entrance on the road side. Wooden floors supported by cast-iron columns. On the Manchester, Bolton and Bury Canal.

High Lane Basin, Canal Street Warehouse

SJ 948 853

18m × 16m, 288m² later 576m², Type 2

Built in 1830s by the canal company. Two storey, stone, warehouse, 3 bays × 4 bays, of two phases. First phase was built in watershot stone. The warehouse was later raised to two storeys, and this phase is in coursed stone. Tall windows with stone sills and lintels. Single, central, loading bay on the canal (eastern) side. Coped gables with locking kneelers and a twentieth-century thin slate roof. Internal floors of wood supported by wooden beams and cast-iron columns. There are cottages abutting the northern elevation. On the Macclesfield Canal.

Hyde Wharf

SJ 943 951

13.5m × 16m, 648m², Type 3

Built 1828 by the canal company. On the eastern side of the Peak Forest Canal is a fine brick-built warehouse, three storeys terraced into the hillside with only two storeys on the road side, 5 bays by 3 bays,

The ruins of the Grocer's warehouse.

semi-circular arched windows, central opening in road front blocked, loading opening on canal front with windows each side. On the Peak Forest Canal.

Leigh, Canal Street Warehouse I

SJ 655 998

15.2m × 10.8m, 328m², Type 2

Built 1821 by canal company. Warehouse with counting house is watershot stone built, of two storeys, 7 × 3 bays. Western two bays form the counting house, now a cottage. Thick slate pitched roof. Taking-in doors on canal and road side. Wooden floors supported by transverse beams and timber posts. On Leigh branch of Leeds and Liverpool Canal.

Leigh, Canal Street Warehouse II

SJ 656 998

17.3m × 13.1m, 680m², Type 3

Built 1894 by canal company. Brick built warehouse at eastern end of original building. Three storeys, 5 bays × 5 bays. Roof has queen-post trusses and is laid with thin slates. Small engine house on ground floor to power the hoists. Taking-in doors to each floor on canal and road side with cathead cranes above. On Leigh branch of Leeds and Liverpool Canal.

Manchester, Kenworthy Warehouse

SJ 830 976

19m × 47m, 5358m², Type 1

Built 1840s, six storey brick building. Situated on a canal arm to the north-east of Giant's Basin it was enveloped by the viaduct for the Great Northern Railway in 1897. Demolished in the mid-twentieth century, although some of the foundations including part of the flagged floor and its two internal canal arms can still be seen. Castlefield Basin.

Manchester, Merchant's Warehouse, Castlefield Basin

SJ 831 975

46.2m × 15.4m, 2846m², Type 1

Built *c.* 1827–8. Four storeys, brick-built, with on the street side six loading bays crowned by wooden hoods (catheads) containing the hoists. Between the loading bays are five pairs of semi-circular arched windows. The river side has twin shipping holes with mezzanine floor above. Damaged by fire but since rebuilt and converted into offices.

Manchester, Middle Warehouse

SJ 832 974

65m × 19m, 6175m², Type 1.

Built 1831 by canal company. Castlefield Basin. Brick built warehouse of five storeys, plus attic. Two large shipping holes, set within a massive blind arch, front the Middle Basin, a short canal arm which ran off the River Medlock. It has the small, round-arched windows typical of late Georgian warehouses. Converted to offices and flats.

Manchester, Grocers' Warehouse

SJ 832 975

19.4m × 9.7m, 940m², late addition 81m × 9.6m, 3888m², Type 1

Built 1770–78 by canal company and later private company. Castlefield Basin. Five storey brick warehouse (but only four visible at the Castle Street level) cut into the cliff face. Designed by James Brindley it used an internal water-wheel fed from the river to power the hoist system. The original warehouse (which stood 45 feet or 13.7m high) had a single shipping hole running right through the middle of the building into a tunnel behind. Extensively rebuilt in 1800, when it was doubled in size, and again in

Manchester, Castlefield, Merchant's Warehouse with the Middle Warehouse in the background.

1807 when a second boat hole was added. Largely demolished in 1960. However, the first floor survives, along with the rebuilt boat holes, and most of the northern wall and parts of the eastern end of the later extension, which can be seen on the eastern side of the Knott Mill Bridge where the walls survive up to two storeys.

Manchester, Duke's Warehouse

SJ 833 974

23m × 22m, later additions 14m × 22m and 34m × 14.5m, 2024m², later 5228m², Type 1.

Built *c.* 1770–71 by canal company. Extensively rebuilt in 1789 after a fire. Destroyed by fire in 1919. Four phased, four storey, brick warehouse. Primary phase being the central square block straddling the River Medlock with two internal shipping holes. Phases two to four were built in 1778–85 and incorporated the old fulling mill on the southern bank of the Medlock and the old cottages on the northern bank of the Medlock. Only the platform cut into the sandstone cliff on the northern side of the River Medlock (at the terminus of the Bridgewater Canal at Knott Mill Bridge) remains. Recently built over. Located in Castlefield Basin.

Manchester, Victoria and Albert Warehouses, Water Street

SJ 830 981

19.5m × 57m and 19.5m × 20.4m, 7547m², Type 2

Built 1840s. Built by Mersey and Irwell Navigation company at the junction of the Irwell and Manchester and Salford Junction Canal on the site of the old quay. Five storey, L-shaped, brick built warehouse complex with small shall arched windows, and loading openings with cathead crane on both river front and on the canal side, where it was set back. There was direct loading from boats on the riverside where the warehouses were built flush with the river bank. The Albert Warehouse has two loading entrances opening into a courtyard facing Water Street, whilst the Victoria had one flush with Water Street.

Manchester, Great Northern Warehouse

SJ 836 978

81m × 66m, c.26,730m², Type 1

Built 1895–98 by the Great Northern Railway Company. Provided road, rail and canal

Manchester, Victoria and Albert Warehouses.

interchange of five storeys. Goods station at two levels inside warehouse, four platforms and turntables at each level, connected by inclines with hydraulic haulage, marshalling yards to south, approach viaduct from CLCL tracks. Hoists to canal below. External elevations are in the Italianate style. Internal structure of steel pillars, lengthwise and crosswise riveted steel beams and brick jack arches. Over the Manchester and Salford Junction Canal.

Manchester, Dale Street (Salt) Warehouse

SJ 847 982

17.9m × 24m, 2148m², LB2*, Type 1

Built 1806 by canal company. Stone built, five storey warehouse, cut into the hillside so that the western elevation is only four storeys. Loading openings in south wall, two large shipping holes at basement level on east, internal structure of two rows of cast-iron pillars on each floor, side brackets supporting timber beams. Hoists formerly worked by waterwheel built in 1824. Cathead crane on southern gable. Western side of the Rochdale Canal terminus.

Manchester, Tariff Street Warehouse

SJ 848 983

51.4m × 17.1m, 4395m², Type 1

Built 1836 by the canal company. Five storeys, brick-built, austere facades with small semi-circular arched windows. Single arched shipping hole in the southern elevation. Cathead cranes on southern elevation. Northern side of the Rochdale Canal terminus.

Marple, Macclefield Canal Wharf

SJ 961 884

9.5m × 14m, 266m², Type 1

Built 1830s by the Macclesfield Canal Company. Two storey, 3 bays × 5 bays, stone-built warehouse with coped gables and locking kneelers, stone-flag roof and stone steps leading to the first floor at eastern end. There is a two storey cart and loading bay in the western gable with wooden lintels. Unusually the warehouse runs parallel to the canal and there is a single boat hole running the full length of the warehouse on the canal side (as at Bury Wharf). The floor is supported by wooden beams and posts. Near the junction of Peak Forest and Macclesfield Canals.

Marple, Samuel Oldknow's Warehouse

SJ 962 890

22m × 10m, 660m², Type 1

Built 1801–5 by the canal company. Three storeys, 3 bays by 7 bays. Stone-built warehouse with pitched stone-flag roof, internal canal arm on the western elevation running parallel to the canal. There is also a parallel cart entrance. Both have keystone arches. Semi-circular arched windows to all elevations. There is a central loading opening in bay 4, with cathead cranes on both the canal and roadside elevations. The southern gable, with its second floor cart entrance, is built into the hillside and only rises two storeys above the roadside. Internal wooden floors supported by beams and timber posts. Queen post roof. Remains of hand-powered chain hoist in roof truss, with cast-iron roller, operated by large handwheel. Warehouse converted to offices in 1976. By Lock 10 of the Peak Forest Canal.

Stalybridge, Melbourne Street

SJ 964 983

9m × 6m, 216m², Type 3

Built 1820s. Four storey brick-built warehouse on the northern side of the Huddersfield Canal. Loading doors and hoists still present on the southern, canal side, of the building. On the Huddersfield Canal.

Stalybridge, Cornmill Site

SJ 966 985

9m × 18m, 486m², Type 3

Built *c.* 1840 by the canal company. Three storey, stone built warehouse on the northern side of the Huddersfield Canal. Loading doors on the southern canal side. Cart loading entrance on the western side of the building. On the Huddersfield Canal.

Stockport, Wharf Street Warehouse

SJ 893 912

14m × 41m, 574m², Type 1

Built 1798 by the canal company. Three storey, brick, warehouse in EGW bond, running parallel to the canal, with round-arch headed windows to all elevations. Internal canal arm in the northern most bay with round-arched entrance way. Partially demolished. Only the northern and western walls survive to second floor height, the northern gable being cut into the hillside so that only the third second and third floors were visible. Occupied by C.A.L. Tyres Ltd but site owned by British Waterways. At the Stockport end of the Ashton Canal.

Wigan, Terminal Warehouse, Wallgate Basin

SD 578 053

19m × 21m, 1197m², Type 1

Built *c.* 1777 by the canal company. At the end of the canal arm is a stone-built, almost square, terminal warehouse, three storeys, with twin shipping holes for boats to enter, loading openings above and on Pottery Road and Wallgate fronts. On the Leeds and Liverpool Canal.

Wigan, Terminal Warehouse.

Wigan, Wallgate Basin I

SD 577 052

24m × 16m, 1152m², Type 2

Built *c.*1880 by the canal company. Three storey, 5 bays × 2 bay, brick-built warehouse with attic and slate roof and coped gables with kneelers. Arched windows, surrounded

Lancashire

Blackburn, Eanam Wharf I

SD 688 281, LSMR 2056, LBII

34m × 12m, 816m², Type 2

Built *c.* 1800 by the canal company. A long row of one, two and three-storey stone buildings with large, stone flag roofs. Warehouse I is 6 bays × 2 bays, two storeys, watershot

Blackburn, Eanam Wharf.

by blue glazed brick, and a centrally placed wooden hoist tower projecting over the canal. Wooden floors supported by cast-iron columns. Now a public house. On the Leeds and Liverpool Canal.

Wigan, Wallgate Basin II

SD 576 052

13m × 54m, 2106m², Type 2

Built *c.* 1880 by the canal company. Three storey, 10 bays × 2 bays. Brick-built warehouse with blue-glazed brick banding, stone-flag roof and wooden floors supported by cast-iron columns. Later corrugated iron canopy on wrought-iron supports and two hoist towers projecting over the canal. Late nineteenth-century one-storey brick addition to the east, with projecting canopy supported by wrought iron uprights. Now a visitor centre. On the Leeds and Liverpool Canal.

stone built, with loading bays in the eastern gable and quoins. On the roadside elevation is a cart entrance with a keystone arch. Internally wooden floors supported by cast-iron column. On the Leeds and Liverpool Canal.

Blackburn, Eanam Wharf II

SD 688 281, LSMR 2056, LBII

22m × 15m, 660m², Type 2

Built *c.* 1800 by the canal company. Warehouse II is 3 bays × 3 bays, two storeys built of watershot stone. It has a segmental arch entrance and two 3-light stone-mullioned windows on each floor. There is a projecting cast-iron and wooden loading canopy on the canal side. Internally, wooden floors supported by cast-iron column. On the Leeds and Liverpool Canal.

Blackburn, Eanam Wharf III

SD 688 281, LSMR 2056, LBII

14m × 14m, 196m², Type 4

Built *c.* 1890 by the canal company. Single storey, open-sided, wrought-iron shed, of 5 bays × 3 bays, with hoists in the roof space. There is a projecting wrought-iron and wooden loading canopy on the canal side. On the Leeds and Liverpool Canal.

Blackburn, Eanam Wharf IV

SD 688 281, LSMR 2056, LBII

24m × 13m, 936m², later addition 13m × 13m, 507m², Type 2

Built *c.* 1840 and 1890. Three-storey stone building with large stone flag roof. First phase has 3 bays × 3 bays, second phase has 2 bays × 3 bays. Small-paned windows with shallow stone arches and centrally opposed cart entrances with keystone arches. Projecting loading canopy over the canal side and a three storey wooden hoist tower, centrally placed in the first phase. Wooden floors supported by cast-iron columns. On the Leeds and Liverpool Canal.

Burnley, Dugdale Wharf

SD 815 326, LSMR 6837 LBII

18m × 11m, 396m², Type 2

Built *c.* 1800. Two storey, 4 bays × 3 bay, watershot stone warehouse with quoins and a two bay, two storey, stone cottage attached to the southern elevation. Rectangular structure running parallel to the canal with a gabled two-window symmetrical east front with a central loading door and a loading bay above. There are arched loading bay doors in the eastern most bay fronting the canal. In the right-hand corner is the shaft for a still working wooden jib crane. Interior has two rows of cast-iron columns on

the ground floor only and three queen-post roof trusses. A crane beam survives in the north-western corner of the building.

Burnley, Finsley Gate Boat Yard (Mile Wharf)

SD 843 319, LSMR 16970 LBII

20m × 6m, 240m², Type 2

Built *c.* 1800. Two storey, 5 bays × 3 bays, stone-built warehouse with graduated stone-flag roof, two arched loading openings in bay 3 with a shallow key-stone arch. Gables have kneelers set back from the canal. There is also a dock at the side of the Leeds and Liverpool Canal.

Burnley, Manchester Road Wharf I

SD 8387 3228, LSMR 16790 LBII

33 × 12m, 792m², Type 3

Built 1801. Part of a three warehouse complex. Rectangular, two-storey, stone warehouse of 7 bays × 3 bays with a graduated stone slate roof. The western two bays were occupied by an office. There are original keystone arched cart loading entrances with loading bays above in bays 3 and 7 and a later cart entrance in bay 5. The interior has a wooden floor supported by chamfered timber posts. Now used as a public house. On the southern side of the Leeds and Liverpool Canal.

Burnley, Manchester Road Wharf II

SD 8385 3235, LSMR 16790 LBII

20.4m × 15.6m, 318m², Type 4

Built 1890s. Part of a three warehouse complex. Single storey, open-fronted, stone warehouse, of 3 bays × 5 bays. Roof supported by four rows of full-height cast-iron columns. On the canal side there is a wooden canopy on cantilevered cast-iron columns.

Rear has two wagon doors. Irregular, trapezoidal, plan filling the gap between the earlier Manchester Road Wharf Warehouses I and II. On the southern side of the Leeds and Liverpool Canal.

Burnley, Manchester Road Wharf III

SD 8383 3232, LSMR 16790 LBII

22.6m × 12m, 1085m², Type 2

Built 1841–4. Part of a three warehouse complex. Stone built, four storey warehouse aligned parallel to the canal with rusticated quoins and a slate roof. On the road side there is a central three storey projecting wooden loading bay, supported on cast-iron columns, with a one storey canopy to the south also supported on cast-iron columns. On the canal side there is a central keystone arch loading bay and a wooden canopy on cantilevered cast-iron columns. The interior has wooden floors supported by cast-iron columns and queen post truss roof. Originally only two storeys, the upper two storeys and the wooden canopies were added later, perhaps when Warehouse III was built. There is a later three storey, 2 bay × 1 bay, wooden extension on the eastern elevation. Now used as offices. On the southern side of the Leeds and Liverpool Canal.

Burnley, Healey Wood Road Warehouse

SD 838 321

22.5m × 9.75m, 878m² (later addition 21m × 9.75, giving a total area of 1901m²), Type 3

Built 1801 and mid-nineteenth century. Two phased warehouse built and used by a worsted manufacturer. Primary, eastern wing, which is stone built with quoins and a graduated stone slate roof, has 2 bays × 7 bays and four storeys. There are a series of loading bays to each floor in the central bay 4 on the canal side. The second phase western

wing is also stone built with quoins, but has 2 bays × 6 bays and is of five storeys. Interior has wooden floors supported by wooden and cast-iron columns.

Burscough Wharf

SD 443 122, LSMR 9216

25.4m × 10m, 500m², Type 2

Built 1880s by canal company. Located on the northern side of the canal. Two-storey machine brick-built warehouse with glazed brick detailing, small arched windows and two sets of loading openings on canal front, with a centrally placed hoist. Now converted to cottages. On the Leeds and Liverpool Canal.

Church Wharf

SD 742 285, LSMR 5145 LBII

15.65m × 7.8m + 8.85m × 24.5m, 1343m², Type 1

Built 1836. On the southern bank of the canal. L-shaped, four storey, stone building. The southern road side has two gables linked by a short range which contains a giant arch with rusticated voussoirs and a second floor window. There are 3-tiered round-arched loading doors in the side and gable walls of the end bay. Internal timber floors supported by cast-iron columns. Jib crane at the

Burscough Wharf.

Church Wharf.

north-western corner of the warehouse. On the Leeds and Liverpool Canal.

Enfield Wharf I, Clayton-le-Moors

SD 747 304, LSMR 5156 LBII

43.7m × 9.25m, 808m², Type 2

Built 1801–2. Warehouse and office on the western side of the canal. Coursed sandstone with roofs slates, L-shaped in plan. The warehouse has 8 bays (two are later additions), two storeys with opposed wide double-tier loading bay in the third bay and similar but smaller doors in the later eighth bay. There are 3-light flat mullion windows to both floors. Jib crane at north-eastern corner. On the Leeds and Liverpool Canal.

Enfield Wharf II, Clayton-le-Moors

SD 748 304

19m × 6m, 228m², Type 2

Built 1801–2. Two storey stone warehouse at right-angles to the eastern bank of the canal. This gable end has two loading bays, one above the other. Quoins and three light flat mullioned windows. Graduated thick stone slate roof. Three loading bays on the southern elevation. Jib crane at the south-eastern corner. On the Leeds and Liverpool Canal.

Foulridge

SD 888 426

13.7m × 10.4m, 143m², Type 2

Built *c.* 1800. Two storey stone warehouse, set back but lying parallel to the canal of 3 bays × 1 bay. Central cart entrances in both long elevations. On the Leeds and Liverpool Canal.

Hest Bank, Slyne-with-Hest

SD 470 664, LSMR 15893 LBII

7m × 16m, 224m², Type 3

Built 1820. On the eastern side of the Lancaster Canal. A stone built, two storey, warehouse with slate roof and loading bay in the middle of the canal side elevation and tall windows. The south-east elevation has two doorways

Enfield Wharf I.

Enfield Wharf II.

Hest Bank.

Tarleton Wharf.

with projecting cathead hoods. There is a large cart entrance in both the northern and southern gables, the latter having a datestone which reads '1820'. Single span, timber, floors.

Lancaster, Clayton Bridge House

SD 481 616

12.7 × 4m, c. 102m², Type 3

Built pre-1876 probably as a private warehouse. Two storey stone warehouse, with quoins and tall windows, now converted into a house. Loading bay with cathead on the canal side. Single span wooden floors.

Nelson Wharf

SD 856 381

51m × 14m, c. 2142m², Type 3

Built 1890. Three storey machine brick warehouse of 10 bays × 3 bays with corrugated roof supported by steel trusses and columns. Stone foundations with quoins and decorated cornice below eaves. Tower hoist in bay 2 and pent over the canal. Timber floors on cast-iron columns. Jib

crane at north-western corner. On Leeds and Liverpool Canal.

Parbold Wharf

SD 491 105

14m × 14m, 490m², Type 2

Built *c.* 1800. Watershot stone warehouse of two and a half storeys, 4 bays × 4 bays, with three loading openings on the canal side above which was a hoist, quoins and a catslide roof. On the Leeds and Liverpool Canal.

Tarleton, Bank Bridge Warehouse

SD 459 202, LSMR 10660 LBII

21.7m × 7.5m, 488m², Type 3

Built *c.* 1790. On the eastern side of the canal. Rectangular warehouse of 2 bays × 5 bays and three storeys built of red, EGW, bond brick with sandstone dressings and slate roof. Sides and gables have loading bays and the southern gable is terraced by one storey into the hillside. Interior has timber posts supporting a timber floor. Built to serve the Leeds and Liverpool Canal 'new cut' from Burscough to Tarleton.

Merseyside

Liverpool, Pall Mall

SJ 340 915

27m × 18m, 2430m², later 100m × 18m, 1800m², Types 2 and 4

Built *c.* 1840 and *c.* 1880 on the western side of the canal (now filled in) by the canal company. The centre piece of this large complex is a five storey brick warehouse with quoins and internally cast-iron columns and fire proof brick vaulting. This is flanked by a later range of one storey brick warehouses, with steel truss roofs and cast-iron columns built in the 1880s. On the Leeds and Liverpool Canal.

Pall Mall.

Liverpool, Bankhall

SJ 343 936

32m × 18m, 3456m², Type 1

Built *c.* 1840 on the western side of the canal by the canal company. Six storey brick warehouse with segmental brick arches above windows, an internal canal arm and terracing on the road side. Internally there are wooden floors with cast-iron columns. There is a later open-side shed with a canopy over the canal. On Leeds and Liverpool Canal.

Bankhall.

Glossary

ashlar — cut stone, with a very smooth surface.

Bay — a building division, usually determined by the position of major cross-walls or roof trusses

cathead canopies — projecting wooden roof covering a hoist.

catslide — a steep, continuous, roof that covers both the main building and a one storey lean-to addition.

Cruck truss — a timber truss comprising two large curved timbers, known as crucks or blades, jointed at the apex. A cruck truss is effectively a roof truss which is structurally independent of the side walls of a building. Cruck-framed buildings were a common structural form during the medieval and early post-medieval periods.

EGW — English Garden Wall bonded brick.

Headrace and tailrace — the artificial channels dug to bring water to a water wheel (the head-race) and take it away (tailrace).

Just-in-time working — where the amount of stock held by any business is kept to the absolute minimum.

Keystone — the central stone in an arch, which is larger than the other composite stone of the arch and sometimes decorated. Its function of holding the arch together gives rise to its name.

kneeler — a decorative stone projecting from the corner of a gable.

penstock — small tank above a waterwheel which is used to help control the water flow over the wheel.

Quoins — stone blocks sued to strength the exterior corners of a building. Very popular from the seventeenth to the nineteenth centuries.

Single-depth — a term used of a building which is only one room deep.

Truss — a main structural component of a roof. All other elements of a roof are supported by the truss.

Canal and Waterways Museums to Visit

North West Museums

Portland Basin Museum, Portland Place, Ashton-under-Lyne, OL7 0QA. The museum is open daily (except Mondays) from 10am to 5pm and admission is free. Tel 0161 343 2878.

The Boat Museum, South Pier Road, Ellesmere Port, Cheshire, L65 4FW. Tel 0151 355 5017.

Eanam Wharf Visitor Centre, Eanam Wharf, Blackburn, BB1 5BL. Tel 01254 56557

Lancaster City Maritime Museum, St George's Quay, Lancaster, LA1 1RB. Tel 01524 64637.

Merseyside Maritime Museum, Albert Dock, Liverpool, L3 4AQ. Tel 0151 207 0001.

Salford Quays Heritage Centre, 3 The Quays, Salford, M5 2SQ. Open Monday to Friday 9am to 4pm. Admission free. Tel 0161 876 5359.

Wigan Pier Heritage Centre and Trencherfield Mill, Wallgate, Wigan, WN3 4EU. Open Saturdays and Sundays 11am to 5pm, Monday to Thursdays 10am to 5pm. Admission charge. Tel 01942 323666.

Other Museums

Basingstoke Canal Centre, Mytchett Place Road, Mytchett, Surrey, GU16 6DD. Tel 01252 370073.

Batchworth Local Canal Centre, 99 Church Street, Rickmansworth, Herts, WD3 1JD. Tel 01923 778382.

Birchills Canal Museum, Old Birchills, Walsall, WS3 8QD. Tel 01922 645778.

The Canal Museum, Stoke Bruerne, Towcester, Northants, NN12 7SE. Tel 01604 862229.

Foxton Canal Museum, Middle Lock, Gumley Road, Foxton, Market Harborough, Leics, LE16 7RA. Tel 0116 279 2657.

Kennet and Avon Canal Museum, Canal Centre, Couch Lane, Devizes, Wiltshire, SN10 1EB. Tel 01380 721279.

London Canal Museum, Battlebridge basin, 12/13 New Wharf Road, Kings Cross, London, N1 9RT. Tel 020 7713 0836.

National Waterways Museum, Llanthony Warehouse, Gloucester Docks, Gloucester, GL1 2EJ. Tel 01452 318054.

Powysland Museum and Montgomery Canal Centre, The Canal Wharf, Welshpool, Powys, SY21 7AQ. Tel 01938 554656.

River and Rowing Museum, Mill Meadows, Henley-on-Thames, Oxfordshire, RG9 1BF. Tel 01491 415600.

Shardlow Heritage Centre, Canalside, London Road, Shardlow, Derby, DE72 2GA.

Union Canal Society, Canal Museum, Linlithgow, West Lothian, EH49 6AJ. Tel 01506 671215.

Waterfolk Canal Museum, Old Storehouses, Llanfrynach, Brecon, Powys, LD3 7LJ. Tel 01874 665382.

Further Reading

Aldred J, 1988, *Worsley, an Historical Geography.* Worsley Civic Trust.

Armstrong J, 1989, 'Transport and Trade', in Pope R, (ed), *Atlas of British and Social and Economic History since c.1700.* London, Routledge, 96–133.

Ashmore O, 1969, *The Industrial Archaeology of Lancashire.* London, David & Charles.

Ashmore, O, 1982, *The Industrial Archaeology of North-West England.* Manchester University Press.

Boucher C T, 1968, *James Brindley, Engineer 1716–1772.* Goose & Son Ltd, Norwich.

Burke T and Nevell M, 1996, *A History and Archaeology of Tameside. Volume 5: Buildings of Tameside.* Tameside Metropolitan Borough with the University of Manchester Archaeological Unit.

Brumhead D and Wyke T, 1997, '"The Duke's Agents Have Made a Wharf". Castlefield and its Warehouses', in McNeil R and George A D, *The Heritage Atlas 3: Warehouse Album.* Field Archaeology Centre, University of Manchester, 26–9.

Brunskill R, 1994, *Timber Building in Britain.* Victor Gollancz, London.

Clarke M, 1990, *The Leeds and Liverpool Canal. A History and Guide.* Carnegie Press, Preston.

Clarke M, 1999, 'British Canal History in Perspective?', *Waterways Journal* Vol 1, 24–36.

Clegg H, 1955, 'The Third Duke of Bridgewater's Canal Works in Manchester', *Transactions of the Lancashire and Cheshire Antiquarian Society,* Vol 65, 91–103.

Cootes R J, 1982, *Britain Since 1700,* 2nd edition. London, Longman.

Cronin P and Yearsley C, 1985, 'Coal Mining in Denton and Haughton', in Lock A, (ed), *Looking Back at Denton.* The Libraries and Arts Committee, Tameside Metropolitan Borough, 58–69.

Crowe N, 1994, *English Heritage Book of Canals.* English Heritage and Batsford, London.

Devle B, 1997, 'Vision into Reality: the Portland Basin renaissance', in McNeil R and George A D, *The Heritage Atlas 3: Warehouse Album.* Field Archaeology Centre, University of Manchester, 50–1.

Fitzgerald R, 1980, *Liverpool Road Station.* RCHME and Greater Manchester County Council. Manchester.

George A D, 1997, 'Housing the Bulk Cargoes: an introduction to canal warehouses', in McNeil R and George A D, *The Heritage Atlas 3: Warehouse Album.* Field Archaeology Centre, University of Manchester, 24–5.

Greene J P, 1995a, 'The 1995 Chaloner Memorial Lecture. The 1830 warehouse and the nineteenth century trade in timber', *Transactions of the Lancashire and Cheshire Antiquarian Society,* vol 90 for 1994, 1–13.

Greene J P, 1995b, 'An archaeological study of the 1830 Warehouse at Liverpool Road Station, Manchester', *Industrial Archaeology Review* 17, 2 (Spring 1995), 117–28.

Hadfield C, 1966, *The Canals of the West Midlands.* The Canals of the British Isles Series, David & Charles, Newton Abbot.

Hadfield C, and Biddle G, 1970, *The Canals of North West England.* Two volumes. The Canals of the British Isles Series, David & Charles, Newton Abbot.

Hadfield C and Boughey J, 1998, *Hadfield's British Canals. The Inland waterways of Britain and Ireland.* Eighth Edition. Sutton Publishing, Bridgend.

Herson J, 1996, 'Canals, railways and the demise of the port of Chester', in Carrington P, (ed),

Where Deva Spreads her Wizard Stream. Trade and the Port of Chester. Papers from a Seminar held at Chester, November 1995. Chester Archaeology Occasional Paper No 3. Chester City Council, 75–89.

Holden B E, 1979, *The Rochdale Canal.* Rochdale Canal Society, Rochdale.

Jones, F M, 1967, 'Liverpool Dock Buildings as Historical Evidence', *Transactions of the Historical Society of Lancashire and Cheshire,* Vol 118, 87–103.

Keaveney E and Brown D L, 1974, *The Ashton Canal. A History of the Manchester to Ashton under Lyne Canal.* Manchester.

Lloyd D W, 1998, *The Making of English Towns.* New Edition. Victor Gollancz Ltd in association with Peter Crawl.

McNeil, R and Nevell M, 2000, *A Guide to the Industrial Archaeology of Greater Manchester.* Association for Industrial Archaeology, Redruth.

Nevell, M D, 1997, *The Archaeology of Trafford. A Study of the Origins of Community in North West England Before 1900.* Trafford MBC with UMAU and GMAU.

Owen D, 1977, *Canals to Manchester.* Manchester University Press.

Paget-Tomlinson E, 1993, *The Illustrated History of Canal and River Navigations.* Sheffield, Sheffield Academic Press.

Peters J E C, 1969, *The Development of Farm Buildings in Western Lowland Staffordshire up to 1880.* Manchester University Press.

Ransom, P J G, 1979, *The Archaeology of Canals. World's Work Ltd.* Tadworth.

RCHME 1996, *Thesaurus of Archaeological Monument Types.* Royal Commission on the Historical Monuments of England, London.

Roberts T W, 1995, *Ellesmere Port – 1795–1920.* New Zealand.

Scattergood D, Ferguson S and Neil N, 1985, 'The Merchant's Warehouse, Castlefield, Manchester', *Greater Manchester Archaeological Journal Vol 1,* 95–8.

Schofield R, 1992, 'Benjamin Outram and the construction of the Ashton Canal', *Lancashire Local Historian Vol 7,* 5–18.

Sillitoe P, 1989, 'Water power and containerisation at Castlefield. Current Investigations into Eighteenth-century Innovative Technology', *Greater Manchester Archaeological Journal* Vol 3 (for 1987–88), 117–8.

Smith P, 1997, *Canal Architecture.* Shire Publications Ltd.

Stratton M and Trinder B, 1997, *English Heritage Book of Industrial England.* English Heritage and Batsford, London.

Tomlinson V I, 1961, 'Early Warehouses on Manchester Waterways', *Transactions of the Lancashire and Cheshire Antiquarian Society* Vol 71, 129–151

Walker J, (ed), 1989, *Castleshaw: the Archaeology of a Roman Fortlet.* The Archaeology of Greater Manchester, volume 4.

Waterson A, 1988, *On the Manchester, Bolton and Bury Canal.* Neil Richardson, Manchester.

Wilkinson S, nd (1980), *Manchester Warehouses. Their History and Architecture.* Neil Richardson, Swinton, Manchester.

Wilkinson P, 2000, *The Shock of the Old. A Guide to British Buildings.* Channel 4 Books, an imprint of Macmillan Publishers Ltd.

Wilson P N, 1968, 'Canal Head, Kendal', *Transactions of the Cumberland and Westmoorland Antiquarian Society and Archaeological Society Vol LXVII (New Series),* 132–50.

Young A, 1771, *A Six Month Tour through the North of England ...* Volume 3. 2nd edition.

Index

Entries in **bold** indicate pages on which figures or plates and their captions occur.